CHILDREN'S PARTICIPATION?

LEARNING FROM CHILDREN AND ADULTS IN THE ASIA-PACIFIC REGION

EDITED BY:
JAN MASON, NATALIE BOLZAN AND ANIL KUMAR

CHILDREN'S PARTICIPATION?

LEARNING FROM CHILDREN AND ADULTS IN THE ASIA-PACIFIC REGION

EDITED BY:
JAN MASON, NATALIE BOLZAN AND ANIL KUMAR

Common Ground

First published in Australia in 2009
by Common Ground Publishing Pty Ltd
at theSocialSciences.com
a series imprint of TheUniversityPress.com

The National Library of Australia Cataloguing-in-Publication data:

Children's Participation?: Learning from Children and Adults in the Asia-Pacific Region
Editors, Jan Mason, Natalie Bolzan, Anil Kumar.

Bibliography.

978 1 86335 688 6 (pbk.)
978 1 86335 689 3 (pdf)

1. Children - Pacific Area.
2. Children's rights - Pacific Area
3. Social Participation - Pacific Area

323.352091823

Front cover designed by Gabrielle Suryaningsih Mason

Table of Contents

Acknowledgments

The editors and members of the Asia-Pacific study group are grateful for the collegial and financial support of the Childwatch International Research Network. This assistance enabled our research to be undertaken and published. We would also like to acknowledge the financial support and assistance of the Social Justice Social Change Research Centre, University of Western Sydney (http://www.uws.edu.au/socialjustice_socialchange/sjsc).

Thanks are also extended to all of the children and adults who kindly gave of their time, in order to enable us to explore children's participation in the region.

Foreword

Two decades since the United Nations Convention of Child Rights and the concept of child participation still leaves us with various connotations of what that actually means. Child participation at the very basic level, to us, exemplifies that children are capable of thought that result in opinions and decisions. What leaves us questioning is the necessary translation of this idea to social policies and their implementations. Can children really participate in decisions that affect their everyday lives? The book chooses to answer and look at these principles of child participation, the role of children in their own decision making as well as the impact of child participation on the community, parents, teachers and others that are involved in the everyday activities of the child. Importantly in answering these questions the book highlights the value of questioning the meanings of the English term 'participation' across cultures and across generations, and of understanding the importance of local, cultural contexts in implementing child participation globally.

Being on the governing board of ChildWatch International (CWI) network for the last decade, I have had the privilege to know the researchers, the research as well as the extensive work that has taken place in bringing together this study. They have included in their work the rich dimensions of the culture along with the complexities of global interaction and influences on families, schools and community networks. With the use of modern technology the children have the opportunity to expose themselves to forums, social interactive websites and other similar environments where their voice matters. They are today aware of their negotiating power with the adult world and have begun to represent themselves in child-centered conferences and other issues related to their population in the region. Children are representing themselves on issues related to climate change, water problems, peace and participating in rehabilitation work. National and international disasters such as the Tsunami invoked child-centered perspectives and needs. It is a challenge to formulate and design a study in these overwhelming contexts in Asia. Researchers from the five countries, China, India, Thailand, Sri Lanka and Australia have put together an impressive body of work highlighting the meaning of child participation from the perspective of children, parents, educators, policy makers and civil society.

Scholars focusing on child participation and child protection have previously looked at the Inter-Agency Working Group document on Minimum Standards for Consulting with Children. "Child Participation?" supports and builds on the findings from Minimum Standards and utilizes the research in a manner that is unique in the region. The book provides insights on privacy for children, personal space from adults as well as inclusion of children's opinions in the adult world. The book stresses that we have no other option but to include children as partners for change. Change for themselves and for others – this viewpoint is a milestone in child research in Asia where adults tend to take the ownership of children's outcomes.

Without drawing on comparisons between the five countries, "Child Participation?" lays out a guideline to work in the field. It provides a ground breaking perspective on changing scenarios in the countries specific to child development and child well-being while drawing out contemporary changes in terms of freedom for children. I hope that researchers will take this book forward and explore the questions that are knowingly raised in this book. I am certain that child right activists, policy makers, child educators and parents would benefit from reading this book and utilizing it towards ensuring that children are accepted and celebrated as partner citizens.

Usha S. Nayar, Ph.D.
Professor, Tata Institute of Social Sciences

Auspicing organisation: Childwatch International

The Childwatch International Research Network is a global, non-profit, nongovernmental network of institutions that collaborate in child research for the purpose of promoting child rights and improving children's well-being around the world. It was founded in 1993 as a response from the research community to the United Nations Convention on the Rights of the Child. The Convention is the basis for the Network's common agenda.

Aims and Ethos

Childwatch links local, regional and national research efforts to an international research-based knowledge, practice and policy on children's issues. It seeks a more effective and strategic approach to child research globally. Childwatch has unique potential to harness the collective capacity of international child researchers to identify and investigate major questions of global significance in the lives of children.

The network focuses on critical issues in the lives of children and youth, and their families. It seeks to encourage multi-disciplinary research, policy development and training that promotes the well-being, rights, civic and social participation, and the full development of children. Childwatch values research about effective and appropriate practices designed to achieve these goals and research that describes the current condition of children and youth. The network celebrates children's capacity to negotiate the realities of their lives in the diverse and often challenging social, political and cultural contexts in which they are growing up. Childwatch promotes understanding of and respect for differences in the cultural norms, values, priorities and challenges of everyday life.

Childwatch understands "child research" as:

- concerning children and young people up to the age of 18 years

- reflecting all the phases and facets of the research process from the formulation of research questions to the dissemination and implementation of findings

- being child-centred, entailing a focus on the child, a holistic view of the child and research approaches that emphasises the participation of children and young people

- being rigorous. It acknowledges the necessary relationship and tension between action and science. Child research must touch closely on children's lives while also living up to the standards of good science

- being inclusive in approach. Child research must oppose gender, ethnic, religious and other forms of discrimination against children.

Childwatch prioritises children in adversity.

Childwatch gives special emphasis to research about children experiencing extreme adversity, including poverty, civil conflict and war, community and family violence, AIDS, trafficking in children, physical displacement, and forced migration wherever these problems exist.

Childwatch aims to promote child rights through child research by:

- raising the profile of child research

- improving resources for child research

- building the capacity of child research institutions through the promotion of collaborative research and research relevant to local contexts.

Chapter 1

Towards Global Acknowledgement of the Child's Right to Participation

Jan Mason and Natalie Bolzan

Introduction

The twentieth century has been referred to as 'the century of the participating child' (Knorth et al. 2002). While the current understanding of the concept of child participation can be traced historically to ideas articulated in the areas of education, community development and human rights, it is predominantly in the theory and practice of education that we find examples of adults advocating children's participation. Since the early 1920s educationalists have promoted children's involvement in schools, both in the dialogic processes of learning and in contributions to the structure and governance of these institutions, where it affected their learning. Educationalists from diverse ideological and national backgrounds have argued the importance of children participating in decision making in schools and communities. These have included Dewey (USA) Makarenko (Russia) Korczak (Poland) Boeke (Holland) Elise Boulding (USA), Maria Montessori (Italy) and AS Neill (Scotland) (De Winter 2002; van Beers et al. 2006). The ideologies espoused by these educationalists meant that they emphasised different aspects of participation, from preparing children for democratic citizenship in the case of Dewey, teaching responsibility for life in socialist communes in the case of Makarenko (1980, cited in De Winter 2002) or, focusing on children's rights as actors and challenging adult oppression of children, in the case of Korczak (1920, cited in de Winter 2002) and AS Neill (1962, cited in van Beers et al. 2006).

The ideas pioneered by these educationalists in the early twentieth century merged with the movement in the later part of the century towards the global codification of universal human rights in international conventions. Bentley (2005) places the movement to global acknowledgement of human rights in the political context of the ending of the Cold War. She argues that the ending of the Cold War was the context which proved the 'impetus for the inception and acceptance' of theUnited Nations Convention on the Rights of the Child (CRC) adopted in 1989, a decade after the International Year of the Child (Bentley 2005, p. 109). It now has the ratification of all countries except the United States.

It was during the drafting of the CRC and then through the activities of the Defence for Children International and UNICEF in seeking to promote the CRC, that the term 'children's participation rights' entered into common use (van Beers et al. 2006). It was during these processes that the notion was introduced that children have rights not just to protection and provision of services, but also to be active in decision making about their own lives and society (Cantwell 1993, cited by van Beers 2006). The focus on child participation as being about acknowledgement of children as actors in their own right, as having agency and the right to have their voices heard has, according to Prout (2000, p. 308), been associated with the two related global social trends of 'democratisation' and individualisation (Fairclough 1992; Prout 2000, citing Beck 1998). These trends, he argues, are characteristic of social structure associated with urban living, particularly in Western countries.

The contemporary definition of 'authentic' participation by children, as reflected in a 2004 UNICEF document, is about starting with children and young people themselves and demanding a change in adult thinking and behaviour, so that adults share with children in determining the way the world is defined. In this context the Convention is generally seen as contributing to the global impetus on child participation and as the benchmark for a change in adult-child relations (eg John 1999). Indeed, it can be argued, with John, that the Convention, with its focus on the child's right to express his or her views, obtain and access information, 'endows the child with a new status in the international arena and poses the research and practitioner community with new challenges' on how to involve children, form partnerships with them and facilitate their agency in their own lives (1999, p. 6). This understanding continues in spite of explicit opposition to signing the Convention within the United States and to implementing it elsewhere.

The origins of our Asia-Pacific research study

The idea for the study on which this book is based: child participation in five countries in the Asia-Pacific region—China, India, Thailand, Australia and Sri Lanka—originated at a meeting of Childwatch International Research Network (CWI). CWI is 'a global, non-profit, nongovernmental network of institutions that collaborate in child research for the purpose of promoting child rights and improving children's well-being around the world. It was founded in 1993 as a response from the research community to the United Nations Convention on the Rights of the Child, an instrument for changing the focus of research and for ensuring that the perspectives of children are heard. The Convention is the basis for the Network's common agenda'.[1] CWI has an ongoing focus on the child participation principles of CRC, deciding at its 1999 Board meeting to focus on these principles as a basis for regional network co-operation and in this context to evaluate 'the growing body of international rhetoric and practice concerning children's participation and inclusion in democratic processes' (Proposal for an international Symposium facilitated by CWI and the MOST program of UNESCO). The research organisations in which the study participants in these countries were situated are all members of the Asia-Pacific Network of CWI. Some details of the demographics of these countries, relevant to children, are summarised in the Table following this chapter.

When we commenced the project in 2004, our research revealed only a small amount of material which discussed the conceptualisation of child participation across cultures. This was despite the fact that over a decade ago an Editorial in *Childhood* had acknowledged the importance of 'different concerns and approaches coming out of different world regions' in contributing to more comprehensive knowledge about children's lives and the policies impacting on them (1997, p. 197). As Theis has noted, where there has been documentation of child participation approaches in the Asia-Pacific region, these approaches 'are often written by international agencies or their English-writing consultants' and therefore much of this documentation 'reflects the experiences and priorities of the(se) agencies and individuals' (Theis 2007, p. 12). In our project, we adopted a collaborative or partnership approach whereby all the researchers were embedded in research in their own countries and worked collaboratively across countries at all stages of the research. It was intended that the conduct and reporting of our individual country and collective findings reflect the experiences of representatives of all countries involved in the study: China, India, Thailand, Australia and Sri Lanka.[2]

1.<http://www.childwatch.uio.no/about/> CWI funded inter-country visits to progress the research described in this chapter. The Social Justice and Social Change Research Centre (SJSC) at the University of Western Sydney (UWS) contributed funds for editorial work towards this chapter.

2.Participant countries in this book are generally listed according to population size.

Rationale, aims and methods of study

Rationale and context

In initial discussions amongst study group members we agreed that while child participation was used as a term describing the pertinent UNC principles, rarely were the actual meanings of the term (as used in discussions about implementation within our individual countries) made explicit. As researchers from the five participating countries, we aimed to explore, in our own countries, the meanings being attributed to the concept of child participation. We wanted to discover what was considered appropriate in terms of child participation, to what extent it was being implemented, and what factors were supporting and/or limiting child participation in each of the countries. We agreed we would attempt to conduct this exploration at family, community and policy levels in the five countries. Initially, because of the apparent interconnectedness between participation and citizenship, we also aimed to explore the relationship between the two concepts. We put this aim aside, however, hoping to explore it at a later time in some detail, in collaboration with a concurrent CWI project focusing on the topic of children and citizenship (Taylor and Smith 2009).

Methods

At the beginning of the project it was clear that we lacked the resources required to tackle the considerable problems of implementing comparative research across cultures. We focused, instead, on scoping the area through an approach which would allow us to collaborate and dialogue around the conduct of parallel research in our different countries. We commenced our planning for the research on the basis that we would be applying a partnership approach, attempting to implement very similar research projects in each of the five countries. Limited literature was available to provide guidance on conducting parallel qualitative studies in Eastern and Western countries. The most pertinent example was provided by Easterby-Smith and Malina (1999), which discusses issues in a partnership between researchers in China and the UK around management research. As with the partners in the research discussed by Easterby-Smith and Malina (1999), we discovered very early in the implementation of the project that we had to be flexible around our initial idea of parallel projects.

Our group members decided to use both qualitative and quantitative methods to scope children's participation at levels of family, community and society. Quantitative methods, such as surveys, were to be used where possible and appropriate. Qualitative data would be sought from children, parents, teachers, policymakers and community leaders, through interviews and focus groups and from document analysis and review of legislation, policies, reports and research. The complete data set would be analysed by all country members and we would consider together what the process for and findings from each study meant for the nature of child participation within the Asia-Pacific region.

It became apparent as we proceeded to design the projects that researchers would need to employ methods that fitted with the research agenda of the specific research centres in which they were located. The fact that the research within countries depended on individual country funding and resources made a flexible approach essential. For example, whereas China had large existing projects onto which they could piggyback the participation project, Australian researchers were unable to access new funding and had only a small amount of funding available for this project. Additionally, the researchers in China were able to utilise large samples and had no problems with accessing children, whereas Australian researchers experienced problems in obtaining the support of schools at the local level. The significance of the finding by Easterby-Smith and Malina (1999) of the need to adapt research methods to meet country contingencies, in ways that could not be envisaged in designing the research, was illustrated by fact that the Sri Lankan researcher had access to her sample facilitated by the traumatic tsunami experience. In this instance, children were surviving the tsunami and its aftermath in unstructured situations where it was very easy for them to be accessed and to request their involvement in research. This contrasted strongly with the experience of the Australian researchers who had to approach children through four 'gatekeepers' (the state Department of Education, the local school principal, the classroom teacher and the child's parents). The ease or difficulty of accessing children inevitably influenced unplanned for differences in sample sizes and characteristics.

Ongoing dialogue was a hallmark of the collaboration between members of the network meeting in different countries. The foci of these meetings shifted from discussion of project aims and implementation to analysis and to the way the findings would be written up. Study group members contributed different and complementary skills and knowledge at various stages of the project. Workshops—auspiced by Childwatch International in collaboration with the host countries—took place in Bangkok, Mumbai, Sydney and Beijing, between 2004 and 2006. Meeting in different countries enabled all members to experience some characteristics of the different cultural sites and aspects of the child welfare service provisions in some of the participating countries. These experiences provided invaluable insights into cultural differences, which were then fed into our deliberations. At the broadest level, these experiences contributed to the altered perspectives of individual researchers. They challenged our understanding of the country-specific questions regarding child participation and child welfare. Our attitudes towards conducting research or delivering services became more flexible. As the project progressed, cultural insight became important and cultural contexts impacted on methodological and interpretive approaches, both within and across data. Defining, conducting and discussing our research against the different cultural backgrounds had particular relevance for our understanding of the impact of culture on adult-child relations and on meanings attributed to the concept of child participation.

The workshops also provided opportunities for building what Easterby-Smith and Malina (1999) refer to as the key requisites for effective cross-cultural research—trust and good communications. It became apparent that, in order to avoid the confusion that can arise when participants have different familiarity in the use of a common language, we needed to interrogate the language being used. For example, our common use of the English language camouflaged differences in the way we were using the word 'participation'. While all researchers shared a commitment to a concept of children's participation, we actually had different understandings amongst us of what we meant by the term 'child participation' which paralleled, in some respects, their use in the different national contexts. This was illustrated by understanding that in Sri Lankan, the Sinhala term for participation—'sahabagithvaya'—literally translated means '*to join in with others*'. It has a group emphasis and therefore tends to be contextual and communal in focus. The use of the English word 'participation', while literally meaning 'to take part in', was understood by the Australian participants as having a more individualistic connotation, associated with having the opportunity to express one's views.

In summary, this book is as much about a journey of some 'eastern' and 'western' minds coming to understand each other's attitudes to childhood, as it is about children's participation. The assumptions we brought to the research, our beliefs in what we took to be 'universally' accepted understandings and knowledge, as well as the construction we brought to the notion of 'child', all informed this journey and research. As a result what we provide in this book is a not a single regional picture of children's participation, but a challenge to the concept of a single representation. In the five countries participating in this research—China, India, Thailand, Australia and Sri Lanka—similarities in children's participation were observed, but so also were differences. We did not judge these differences. We simply acknowledge that they exist and propose that any global attempt to impose one framework, set of values or meaning is inappropriate. These similarities and differences are evident in reading the chapters 2–6, which are reports from the individual country studies. They are summarised in chapter seven on the findings. The meanings of what we found in considering the similarities and differences are considered in the final chapter.

References

Beck, U 1998, Democracy Without Enemies. Cambridge, Polity Press

Cantwell, N 1993, 'Monitoring the convention through the idea of the '3 Ps" in Eurosocial Report 45/1993, Vienna: European Centre for Social Welfare policy and Research.

De Winter, M 2002, 'The century of the participating child', in EJ Knorth, PM Van Den Bergh & F Verheij (eds.), *Professionalisation and participation in child and youth care*, Ashgate, England.

Easterby-Smith, M & Malina, D 1999, 'Cross-cultural collaborative research: toward reflexivity', *Academy of Management Journal,* vol. 42, no. 1, pp. 76–86.

Fairclough, N 1992, Discourse and social change, Polity Press, Cambridge.

International child research: promise and challenge, Editorial (1997) *Childhood,* vol. 4, no. 2, pp. 147–150.

John, M (ed.), 1999, *The child's right to a fair hearing,* Jessica Kingsley, London.

Korczak, J 1920, *Jak Kochac Dzieco,* Bijleveld, Utrecht, 1986.

Makarenko, A 1980, *Vortrage uber Kindererziehung,* Volk und Wissen, Berlin.

Neill, A. S 1960, *Summerhill: a radical approach to child rearing.* New York (Hart Publishing Co.)

Prout, A 2000, 'Children's participation: control and self-realisation in British late modernity. *Children & Society,* 14, pp. 304–315.

Taylor, N & Smith, AB (eds.) 2009, *Children as Citizens? International Voices,* Childwatch International Citizenship Study Group, Otago University Press, Dunedin, New Zealand.

Theis, J 2007, 'Performance, responsibility and political decision making: child and youth participation in Southeast Asia and the Pacific' in *Children, youth and environments,* vol. 17, no. 1, pp. 1–13.

UNICEF 2004, *The State of the World's Children,* available as PDF at <http://www.unicef.org/sowc/>.

Van Beers, H, Chau, VP, Ennew, J, Khan, PQ, Long, TT, Milne, B, Nguyet, TT & Son, VT 2006, Creating an enabling environment, Save the Children, Sweden.

r Countries Involved in Childwatch Study

	Year	China	India	Thailand	Sri L
living below $2 U.S. per day [a]	1990–2005	34.9	80.4	25.2	4
living below national poverty line [a]	1990–2004	4.6	28.6	13.6	25
rate (% ages 15 and older)[a]	1995–2005	90.9	61.0	92.6	9
rate (% ages 15 and older) – Female [a]	1995–2005	86.5	47.8	90.5	8
rate (% ages 15 and older) – Male [a]	1995–2005	95.1	73.4	94.9	9
ation growth rate (%)[a]	1975–2005	1.2	2.0	1.3	1
ber of years of schooling (adults)[b]	Latest available	6.4	5.1	6.5	6
r 1000 population)[c]	Latest available	13.5	22.7	13.7	17
er 1000 population)[c]	Latest available	7.0	6.6	7.1	6
ex [a]	2005	0.84	0.62	0.86	0
	Latest available	Han Chinese 91.9% Zhuang, Uygur, Hui, Yi, Tibetan, Miao, Manchu, Mongol, Buyi, Korean, and other nationalities 8.1%	Indo-Aryan 72.0% Dravidian 25.0% Mongoloid and other 3.0%	Thai 75.0% Chinese 14.0% Other 11.0%	Sinhale Sri Lank 7.2% Ind 4.6% Sr Tamil 3. 0.5% Un 10.
	2005	0.703	0.591	0.745	0.
ta (US$)[a]	2005	6,757	3,452	8,677	4,
	2005	81	128	78	9
opment index [a]	2005	0.777	0.619	0.781	0.

	Year	China	India	Thailand	Sri Lanka	A
	Latest available	Standard Chinese or Mandarin (Putonghua, based on the Beijing dialect), Yue (Cantonese), Wu (Shanghaiese), Minbei (Fuzhou), Minnan (Hokkien-Taiwanese), Xiang, Gan, Hakka dialects, minority languages	English enjoys associate status but is the most important language for national, political, and commercial communication; Hindi is the national language and primary tongue of 30% of the people; there are 14 other official languages: Bengali, Telugu, Marathi, Tamil, Urdu, Gujarati, Malayalam, Kannada, Oriya, Punjabi, Assamese, Kashmiri, Sindhi, and Sanskrit; Hindustani is a popular variant of Hindi/Urdu spoken widely throughout northern India but is not an official language	Thai, English (secondary language of the elite), ethnic and regional dialects	Sinhala (official and national language) 74%, Tamil (national language) 18%, other 8%	English 2.1%, Ita 11.1%, u
[a]	2005	72.5	63.7	69.6	71.6	
[a]	2005	0.792	0.645	0.743	0.776	0.931
	Latest available	Daoist (Taoist), Buddhist, Christian 3%–4%, Muslim 1%–2%	Hindu 80.5%, Muslim 13.4%, Christian 2.3%, Sikh 1.9%, other 1.8%, unspecified 0.1%	Buddhist 94.6%, Muslim 4.6%, Christian 0.7%, other 0.1%	Buddhist 69.1%, Muslim 7.6%, Hindu 7.1%, Christian 6.2%, unspecified 10%	Catholic 20.5%, 20.5%, Muslim unspecif
of [c]	Latest available	1.06	1.06	0.98	0.97	

on	2005	1,313.0	1,134.4	63.0	19.1
it rate – ale rate) [a]	1999–2005	na	100	80	216
it rate – our force) [a]	1996–2005	4.2	4.3	1.4	7.7
ion (% of	2005	40.4	28.7	32.3	15.1

an Development Report 2007/2008, United Nations Development Programme, http://hdr.undp.org/en/reports/global/hdr2c
SCO (Accessed through www.nationmaster.com)
World Fact Book, 2007 (Accessed through www.nationmaster.com)

Chapter 2
China

Ju Qing, Chen Chen and Zhao Xia

Introduction

China is a country with a vast territory, a huge population, and a centuries-old history and culture. During the past two decades, reformation and the opening up of trade with the West have allowed China to become one of the fastest developing economies in the world. Chinese society is changing dramatically; its politics and culture have developed exponentially. However, many social problems and conflicts have occurred as a result of this development. The issue of children's participation in China needs to be understood in the context of this complicated background.

Collectivism and individualism

Generally speaking, China is a country based on the idea of a collective and national standard, rather than an individual standard. Traditionally, individuals have not been respected fully, nor have their rights been recognised as important.

China has a two thousand year history as a feudalistic society, with a system ruled by men. According to the ethical code, ruler guided subjects, father guided son, and husband guided wife. Under such a hierarchical society, individuals, particularly children and women, were hardly respected, let alone allowed to participate fully in society.

From the early 1900s, the concept of communism was disseminated throughout China, finally leading to the establishment of the People's Republic of China. The ideology behind communism and socialism is essentially one of collectivism; however, the common people, including children and women, are respected as the owners of the nation and are encouraged to participate in the building up of society.

Subsequent to China's economic development and the increasing adoption of Western conceptions, there is currently a strong trend towards respecting individual rights. At the top level, the central government is carrying out political reformation to promote democracy; at the grass roots level, civil society is becoming more and more active in terms of participation. Children will benefit from this trend, as it has consequently influenced the relationship between adults and minors.

Parents and children

Traditionally, Chinese families were typically patriarchal. The parents, mainly the father, held the authority of guiding their children and deciding all their affairs. This situation has changed dramatically. Due to the policy of family planning carried out in China over a 30-year period, the number of children in each family is reducing. Consequently, children are more and more valued. The relationship between parents and children is becoming equal and parents' 'power' is changing into parents' 'responsibility'. This change in children's position within the family has contributed to their greater participation levels.

Men and women

China has experienced many changes in relation to social sexual role expectations.

The traditional Chinese preference for male children goes back several thousand years. Meanwhile, the doctrines of Women's Three Obedience (to their father before marriage, to their husband after marriage, and to their son after the death of their husband) and Four Virtues (morality, proper speech, modest manners and diligent work) have traditionally guided women's development, particularly that of young girls.

However, in more recent times, the idea of gender equality has started to disseminate throughout China. At present, the people, especially those living in cities, have started to realise that males and females are the same. As a result, more and more people are becoming indifferent to the expectations of social sex roles and there have been greater opportunities for girls to express themselves.

The rich and the poor, the urban and the rural

China's rapid economic development has resulted in some critical problems. One of the more urgent ones is the gap between the rich and the poor, and the urban and the rural.

According to the United Nations Development Program, the current Geordie coefficient for China is 0.45. The people in the poorest quintile account for just 4.7% of China's total consumption, while the people in the richest quintile account for 50% of the country's total consumption. Most of the poor people are now living in rural areas. Because of the distinct economic and social situations, children's participation in urban and rural areas can vary significantly.

Education system

Chinese society is in the process of dividing into various socio-economic classes. For common people, the main way to progress is through the education system, which has an influence on almost every child. Nowadays, exam-oriented education is very serious, and it is becoming more difficult to put forth quality education which is not exam driven. Students are facing increasing study pressures and, as a result, have less time to play and rest. This is a big factor relating to their participation.

Parents often focus much of their attention on children's study. To avoid distraction and to allow children to concentrate on their studies, parents usually do not permit children to participate in housework. Likewise, schools are mainly concerned with students' learning performance and students have limited opportunities to participate in school affairs. Opportunities for children to participate in social affairs are even more limited.

CRC and its implementation in China

The Chinese Government signed the United Nations Convention on the Rights of the Child (CRC) in 1989. The Convention came into effect in 1992.

Since the Convention was ratified by the Chinese Government, the various rights of children have achieved more attention and respect. The government has implemented the fundamental principles prescribed in the Convention by creating a series of laws, policies and administrative measures, and by initiating several child participation projects.

The CRC provides an important reference for the amendment of existing Chinese laws and rules and has become the basis for establishing a Chinese children's law system. The Chinese Government now pursues the principle of child protection and has established a series of laws to protect different aspects of children's rights. In 1991, the Minors Protection Act (MPA) was established. The MPA was the first Act of its kind to exist in

China; it stipulates the respective responsibilities of family, school, society and the justice system in protecting children. Following the introduction of the MPA, similar legislation has been enacted in various provinces and municipalities, and special minors' protection committees or organisations have subsequently been established.

However, the Chinese Government has not stopped at the stage of protection. Instead, it has revised its attitude regarding children as passive objects to be protected to one that regards them as an active main body to be respected. Consequently, changes have been proposed through further Acts and regulations. For example, it is now stipulated in some places that 'children's voices should be listened to' and 'it is necessary to get their consent before implementing a certain measure'. In 2006, the Revised Edition of the Minors Protection Act was passed; this became effective on June 1st 2007. Many issues arising from discussions about the principle of children's participation have been written into the new Act. All of these issues reflect the concept of respecting children.

Regarding policy, the Chinese Government has constituted two Programs for the Development of Children (in 1992 and 2001 respectively) in which children's rights were extended from the right of survival, the right of being protected, and the right of development, to the right of participation. The general aim of the Programs for the Development of Chinese Children from 2001 to 2010 was stated as 'consisting of the principle of "children first", ensuring children's survival right, protection right, development right and participation right, improving children's integrated diathesis, and advancing children's physical and psychological health'. This was the first time that children's participation rights were clearly identified in a Chinese Government document.

The principle of children's participation is increasingly becoming an aspect of Chinese children's rights and it has been ensured and extended widely. A number of organisations in China are now promulgating conceptions and providing children with models for participation. For example, children can now run their own newspapers, their own journals and their own websites. The education model in schools and families is changing from one of indoctrination to a more open and participatory model, which encourages children to participate in activities and makes them the master of their own. Expressions such as "learning from children" and "parents grow up with children" are increasingly being heard. The concept of allowing children to participate in affairs concerning all circles and endowing them with independent human rights has infiltrated into all kinds of child-related work.

The Study

Methods and sampling used in China

Considering the uneven social and economic development of mainland China, as well as its geographic distribution, a stratified sampling method was used. The provinces and municipalities of Zhejiang Beijing, Chongqing, Qinghai, and Liaoning were chosen to represent the southeast, north, southwest, northwest and northeast of China respectively.

For the purposes of the survey, the middle schools of each province or municipality were chosen, with one urban school and one rural school being randomly selected from each area to form the sampling frame for the survey (ten schools in total). As the survey was to be conducted using a focus group methodology, quota sampling was used where needed. For each school, four groups of students were selected: boys aged 12 to 14, boys aged 15 to 17, girls aged 12 to 14, and girls aged 15 to 17. Each group contained six students. Forty-eight students were surveyed in each of the five provinces or municipalities, with 240 students taking part overall. Individual interviews were also conducted with 48 adults, including one teacher and two parents in each school, one community worker and one policy maker in each area, and an additional three national policy makers in Beijing.

Figure 1:Sample distribution

				Zhejiang	Beijing	Chongqing	Qinghai	Liaoning
Urban	Children (120)	12 - 14	Boy	6	6	6	6	6
			Girl	6	6	6	6	6
		15 - 17	Boy	6	6	6	6	6
			Girl	6	6	6	6	6
	Adults (28)		Teacher	1	1	1	1	1
			Parent	2	2	2	2	2
			Community-worker	1	1	1	1	1
			Policy-maker	1	4	1	1	1
Rural	Children (120)	12 - 14	Boy	6	6	6	6	6
			Girl	6	6	6	6	6
		15 - 17	Boy	6	6	6	6	6
			Girls	6	6	6	6	6
	Adults(20)		Teacher	1	1	1	1	1
			Parent	2	2	2	2	2
			Community-worker	1	1	1	1	1

Total children:240

Total adults:48

Findings

Five major and connected themes were drawn from the analysis of the data. These themes are as follows:

1. The meaning of "children's participation"
2. The field of children's participation
3. Participation differences among children of different gender, ages, area and social-economic situations
4. The factors obstructing children's participation
5. The benefits of children's participation.

The majority of the children surveyed understood children's participation to mean taking part in or experiencing something, but neglected to understand it in terms of their position as a main body. A small proportion of the children said that participation meant "to express their views actively" or "to do something with purpose". Very few children thought that participation "is a kind of right". However, most of the adults surveyed understood children's participation to relate to the respecting of children's opinions.

The field of children's participation mainly concentrated on those issues occurring in families and schools that had an effect on children's lives. To some extent, children were able to make decisions about these issues. In comparison, children's participation in community affairs was quite limited and was only discussed by a few survey participants. Some children were even unaware that opportunities for participation existed in the community.

The survey revealed that the extent and depth of participation varied between genders and age groups. Generally, the boys participated more extensively than the girls; older children participated more extensively and deeply than younger children. Comparatively, girls in junior middle school paid more attention to family issues, while girls in senior middle school paid more attention to school issues and boys in senior middle school paid more attention to social issues.

It was also found that children's participation varied across different areas and socio-economic situations. Children in cities had more opportunities to participate and their participation levels in adult affairs were higher than children from rural areas. Children from different socio-economic groups also had different opportunities and channels for participation. Furthermore, children's personalities were a significant factor in their participation levels, with children with active personalities, good expression skills and independent abilities more likely to want to participate and more likely to take an active role in participation.

The following factors were identified by the children as obstructing them from participating: adult's limitation and intervention, individual shortcomings, no channels or opportunities for participation, and traditional conceptions. In contrast, the children identified the following factors as promoting their participation: parents' and teachers' support, personal impulse, and peer encouragement. It is evident that the attitude of adults plays a dual role in children's participation.

Finally, the children identified a range of benefits of participation, including increasing knowledge and capacity, living a happy and colorful life, becoming more confident through expression, becoming more responsible, solving problems, and enabling others to understand children. However, many children also revealed that if their participation is obstructed, they usually feel frustrated and short of self-confidence and courage.

Specific issues regarding children's participation

1. Children's participation in family

Result

Within the family, children's participation can be broken down into three groups: personal affairs, other member's affairs, and common affairs. The results of the children's focus group surveys show that it is more possible for children to play a dominant role concerning their own affairs in contrast to those of other family members. Some children indicated that they could even decide some of their own affairs totally and independently.

Correspondingly, in the adult's interviews, most of the parents expressed that "children could decide by themselves" and "children could decide things together with parents". Only a few parents thought that "children should obey parent's ideas". Pleasingly, it was found that some parents thought that "besides their own affairs, children could participate in other affairs, such as domestic finance and consumption, and their opinions will be respected and considered". Some parents also thought that "children could participate in parents' work and life, and help to coordinate the relationship among family members". However, regarding the aspect of "making friends", most parents were conservative. The proportion of parents with the idea that "children should make friends according to the standard made by their parents" was higher than the proportion maintaining the idea that "children could make friends automatically".

Analysis and discussion

It is really a big improvement that Chinese families are becoming democratic and that, to some extent, children can enjoy participation rights. But there are still problems to be overcome. Further analysis may reveal that the affairs that children are allowed to decide by themselves may be simple and unimportant, such as clothes, entertainment, pocket money, or family activities. It may be that in relation to affairs closer to children's long-term interests, such as friend making, school selection, and vocation choices, it is still the adults who make the decisions.

According to a national investigation on the situation of children's development made by China Youth and Children Research Center in 2005, "school education", "friends" and "entertainment" were the most preferred areas that children wanted to decide independently (64.4%, 35.3% and 35.0% respectively). The results of the investigation were similar to those of our survey, finding that only a small proportion of parents gave children freedom regarding these critical affairs.

It appears that there is a long way for parents to go before they understand and respect their children's rights fully. Moving forward requires further discussion and reflection on the relationship between children's rights of protection and participation.

2. Forbidden area in which only children could participate

Result

When we asked, 'Is there any affair that should be decided by children only, and the adults should not intervene?' we got the following answers: "making friends" and "personal privacy". The children regarded these as "forbidden" areas. Among the different groups, girls in junior middle school and boys in senior middle school put "making friends" in first position, while girls in senior middle school put "personal privacy" in first position.

In contrast, the parents believed that all of children's participation should be directed by adults. Naturally, such oppositional views can potentially lead to conflict.

Many children became emotionally excited when we asked this question. Some of their responses included:

> 'Parents should not open my diary. One's experience and worry are recorded in their diary; therefore nobody else could read it according to the law.' (A boy of junior middle school)

> 'They should not intervene in our affair, because anyway, it is a private thing between us. If they intervene, it will certainly influence our relationships.' (A boy of high middle school)

> 'Privacy is a feeling in our heart, which is the things I don't want my parents to know.' (A girl of senior middle school)

> 'I feel that when children are talking something concerning ourselves, such as early love, the adults should not intervene. We have my own opinions on it, but if the adults are among us, we could not discuss on the topic.' (A girl of senior middle school)

Analysis and discussion

At present, many Chinese parents think it necessary to prevent their children from having boyfriends or girlfriends. They are afraid that such relationships will divert their children's energy away from their studies. But for children, such relationships are a natural development and need, and they dislike their parents' sensitivity about this issue. This situation is just one reflection of the gap between generations.

However, the underlying problem is somewhat more complicated. It is usually a taboo in China for parents to talk about sex issues with children; the same situation applies to teachers in schools. But it is natural that children will be curious about sex; parents' reticence could cause children to become secretive. The different ways in which adults and children approach the issue of sex often lead to children closing the door on their parents.

3. Gender and participation

Result

When we asked the following question, 'Should it be different between boys and girls regarding their participation?' most children answered in the negative:

'I think it was in the past, that some things were limited to man, and other things were limited to woman. But it has been 21st centuries. Men and women are equal now.'

'I feel that there should be no difference, because I have once read a physiological book. It is said that there is no difference between man and women, such as eating, living and so on, all the same.'

However, some children did feel that the participation of boys and girls should be different:

'Regarding participation, I consist on my own opinion. I feel that there should be difference between men and women. Equality is just used to stipulate individual legal status.' (A boy in junior middle school)

'I feel that men and women are different after all. Although it is promulgated that we are equal, but I think women could do as well as men.' (A boy of senior middle school)

'I feel that men and women are born different, as the traditional rule that men furrow and women spin. We are doomed to be different.' (A girl in senior middle school)

But when we asked, 'Are there any differences in daily life?' most of the children gave a positive answer. The adults also answered positively to this question. Many parents thought that boys and girls were not different in their capacity to participate, but that they were different in the fields of their participation. The teachers thought that boys and girls were equal, but that they were different in terms of their participating area. However, the officers thought that the perceived difference between boys and girls regarding participation was not obvious.

In terms of the reasons for a difference in participation, the children identified the following: biological factors, culture and convention, traditional conceptions, personality, and living circumstances.

Analysis and discussion

It is a cause for some optimism that the concept of equality between men and women has been largely accepted, particularly among the coming generation. However, in current practice there is still discrimination between genders.

Children's ideas on this issue are very inspiring. They are not rigid in terms of understanding the equality between women and men. Although some of them are still influenced by traditional social sex role expectations, most of them have their own explanations. To some extent, they are right—we should not understand equality mechanically.

The children expressed their opinions on this issue from their own perspective. They talked about some deep questions, such as equality, traditional conceptions and even legal status. The depth of their thoughts and the perspective of their thinking were commensurate with those of adults. It reinforces the idea that we should believe in children's capacity, and that their voices should be listened to.

4. Age and participation

Result

When we asked, 'Should there be any differences between different age groups in terms of participation?' most of the children gave a positive answer:

> 'Children are facing the same opportunities, but their capacities are different. Different age means different capacity, therefore the participation is different.'

> 'Small children mostly obey their parents, but it is different for older ones.'

When we asked, 'Have you experienced the difference in your life?', most of the children gave a positive answer. Some children said that when they entered primary school, their parents started to ask for their advice, but often didn't accept that advice. However, after they entered middle school or later, their parents paid more attention to their advice, as the parents were more reassured about their behaviour and allowed them to enjoy more freedom.

When we asked, 'At what age should children decide their own affairs?' only one girl in junior middle school told us 'We start to participate once we were born.' A small proportion of children expressed that children could decide their own affairs from primary school age. About one quarter of the children believed that children could decide their own affairs once they started middle school. But most of the children thought that they could decide their own affairs once they reached 18 years. Many of them thought this was because they would take exams for college and university at the age of 18, after which they would leave their families and parents to start their independent lives.

Analysis and discussion

Children have the right of participation once they are born, but in China, most children don't realise this. They confuse the right to participate with becoming an adult at 18 years. This is a problem that needs some immediate attention. As discussed earlier, the Chinese Government has taken the first steps towards recognising participation rights through the promotion of children's rights in our legislation and policy. However, it appears that there is a long road ahead before the average person fully understands this concept.

5. Factors obstructing children's participation

Result

In terms of factors that obstruct their participation, the children identified the following: adults' limitation and intervention, individual shortcomings, no channels or opportunities for participation, and traditional conceptions. The adults gave a range of opinions: teachers thought that lack of time was the main factor; parents thought their ignoring of children's ideas was the main factor; and the community workers thought that lack of funds was the main factor.

When we asked children for ideas on how to improve their participation, they gave us the following suggestions: adults' encouragement, improvement of individual capacity, adults' willingness to listen to their ideas, increasing channels and opportunities for participation, and greater social support.

Analysis and discussion

From the children's answers, we found that limitation and intervention from adults is the biggest obstacle in terms of children's participation. The adults also recognised their own attitudes and conceptions as significant obstructing factors regarding children's participation. However, children and adults ranked the factors differently. Children viewed the limitation of parents and teachers as the main factor obstructing their participation whereas the adults viewed "lack of time" or "lack of funds" as the main factors. Further analysis is needed to understand these different positions and to determine which one is more accurate.

Many adults are critical regarding the realisation of children's rights of participation. As the children suggested, in order to realise their participation, children need adults to listen to their voices, to provide them with channels, and to cultivate in them the capacity for participation. Therefore, adults must take responsibility for developing these factors to promote children's participation.

Limitations and conclusion

In this survey, the rural regions were in fact the suburbs between the urban and the rural areas. Therefore, there are indicator limitations in comparable variables. In addition, the measure of socio-economic status has not been clearly defined. The conception of "middle-class" is defined according to the researchers' perception and is therefore not impartial.

In spite of the shortcomings outlined above, this survey shows the situation of children's participation in mainland China. Adults' attitudes and policy-makers' conceptions are gradually improving. As China continues to open to the world and to strengthen democratic conceptions, children's self-decision and independence, along with their understanding of and desire for participation, will increase accordingly. However, whilst ideas and attitudes have started to change, it could take some time for them to become common practice.

A child's desire and ability to participate relies on adult cultivation and advocacy. Children will always be the "silent" group unless the whole society is willing to hear their voices and to give them opportunities to express them. In our interviews with the children, many of them were unable to express their feelings and views. Because of the long-term compulsory infusion of some values by adults, some children cannot express themselves in their own language or may hide their real feelings.

Children care about themselves, their families and their society. The question of children's participation is not merely one of possessing rights, protecting rights and exerting rights. In fact, it is concerned with the integrated and healthy development of children. Its existence is a symbol of maturity for a democratic society. We need to bridge the gap between research and policy-making processes so as to promote the realisation of children's participation nationwide.

Chapter 3
India

Usha S. Nayar and Anil Kumar

Introduction

Since its emergence in the late 1970s, the notion of 'participation' has become widely acknowledged as a basic operational principle of development programming. To some, it is a means to an end; a process whereby local people co-operate or collaborate in an externally introduced project. To others, it constitutes an end in itself, with the goal being to help people acquire the skills, knowledge and experience to take more responsibility for their own development and, ultimately, be enabled or empowered to transform their lives and their environment.

Until the early 1990s, the word 'participation' was oriented towards adult-focused activities and was activated at the community level through the use of tools associated with Participatory Rural Analysis (PRA). The Convention on the Rights of the Child (CRC), which was adopted by the United Nations in 1989 and which has been ratified almost universally since then, has provided vital encouragement towards the greater participation of children by governmental and non-governmental organisations (Ackerman et al. 2003). CRC implicitly guarantees the participation of children in all decisions concerning them and is the first international instrument that strongly advocates for the participation of children and their right to form associations. The current importance of child participation has emerged from the 2003 version of the highly influential UNICEF report titled *The State of the World's Children*, which took child participation as its theme. An important finding of this report was the notion that the mere act of participation does not qualify the nature or quality of that participation.

In most Asian societies, children, because of their physical and mental immaturity, are almost totally dependent on adult structures of political and economic power to safeguard and protect their rights and well-being. This situation of dependence and vulnerability is often exploited by those with responsibility over children in the name of economic expediency, culture or tradition. Children are effectively viewed as property whose individual rights must be subsumed in the interests of family, community and authority. The scale and diversity of South Asia presents the governments of the region with a huge challenge in implementing the CRC and other international human rights standards. All of these governments face problems of institutional weakness and resource constraints; some are dealing with difficult internal security situations or conflicts, while others are facing entrenched social attitudes and practices. The CRC recognises this and emphasises "international cooperation" to end abuses and promote development. Many articles, such as those relating to education and health, underline this need and the Committee on the Rights of the Child has been empowered to help mobilise international resources to this end.

It is during childhood that individuals form their view of the world and how to act within it. If children are socially and economically marginalised, and acquainted only with poverty, hardship, discrimination and abuse, these experiences will shape them as adults. If, on the other hand, society ensures the freedom and dignity of children, creating the conditions in which they can develop their potential, they will have the chance to grow to a full and satisfying adulthood and to assume a constructive role in society. In South Asia, children make up over 40% of the population—around 539 million of more than 1.2 billion people are under 18 years old—with 13.3% of the total number being under the age of five. Children in South Asia constitute a quarter of the world's children. Economic disadvantage, social exclusion and political marginalisation, combined with the vulnerability of age, perpetuate cycles of abuse in this region.

Girl children face particular disadvantages in the South Asian context. The persistence of discriminatory attitudes towards girls means that the birth of a girl is often considered a liability to a family and less is invested in her health and education. In many countries, gender-selective abortion and infanticide are common and girls figure disproportionately in infant mortality and illiteracy statistics. These factors, together with the persistence of harmful practices such as dowry and child marriage, also feed other cycles of abuse, including domestic violence and sexual exploitation.

India's historical contexts and their relevance for child participation

This section attempts to summarise the historical contexts in India that still have a strong bearing on shaping child participation in the country. In India, religion has a tremendous role in defining, limiting and supporting the participation of children in various spheres. Migration from foreign countries, both through invasion and through trade migration, has resulted in the formation of a large number of religions in India. It is essential to keep in mind that these religions have traditionally differed in the opportunities they provide to children in terms of socialisation and therefore participation. The different approach of each religion to children's involvement continues even today and results in different opportunities for participation.

A closely related factor that has influenced the scope of child participation has been the creation of social classes based on the economic division of society into occupational categories. Subsequent to the migration from middle Asia, India's people were artificially divided into two categories: Aryans and the native Dravida. The establishment of Aryans in India also saw the division of people according to the occupation they were engaged in, resulting in the creation of four main caste groups: Brahmin, Kshatriya, Vaisya and Shudra. Over the course of time, this division was woven into the societal fabric and thus became the essential criteria for ascertaining the social status of an individual. The success of the upper class in dividing the society into occupational groups (with their necessary relation to economic status) has resulted in marked variations in the living standards of various groups. This has limited the opportunities available to children belonging to certain groups, as children from a particular caste are often only allowed to interact closely with children of the same or higher caste. The variations in opportunities available to children are also linked to cultural differences regarding the perception of childhood which are, in part, produced and regulated by the existence of caste and sub-caste groups.

Until the twentieth century, Indian society was characterised by the existence of a joint and extended family system. In this system, a family consisted of people from various generations. Children were viewed as a group to be protected, and there was an expectation that they would grow up as 'good' children. The extended family system supported this expectation by providing ample scope for interaction with older generations and was thus conducive to the 'inheritance' of family and community values down through the generations. This was important, as opportunities for children to socialise outside of the family were limited.

The beginning of the twentieth century witnessed massive migration from southern India to foreign countries, due to people searching for employment. Over time, this situation motivated others in the region and elsewhere in India to migrate to other countries, or to areas within each region or state. The living standards and the new ideas these migrants brought from their place of origin had an impact on the aspirations of others, creating an atmosphere conducive to the nuclearisation of families. The process of nuclearisation of families was primarily based on a concept of individualism or growth of individual families, and the major aim was self-centered growth rather than societal welfare. This process resulted in the adoption of values that are characteristic of an individualistic society; in such a society, children are often socialised to believe that success as an adult is primarily based on materialistic notions.

Educational development is another factor that has influenced the opportunities for participation. Traditionally, the percentage of children attending regular formal education was very low and this had an effect on the extent of their participation. However, the out-of-school children had other opportunities to participate in various activities that school-going children didn't have. Now that access to education has improved across the country, differences in the type and extent of participation can be observed between rural and urban children, as well as those that attend school and those that don't.

There are also differences in participation related to the different ways that children are socialised according to their gender. Traditionally, girl children were confined to the house and socialisation was limited to those avenues that would make them good housewives in the future. Therefore, girls did not get as many opportunities to participate as boys did. The general view was that it was not necessary to educate girl children beyond a basic level. The preference for sons still exists in many parts of India and this also has an influence on girl children's participation. In families with a preference for sons, the avenues for participation are severely limited for girl children, whereas in families without any preference (or which have a preference for girl children), the avenues are far greater.

The National Policy for Children in India was formulated in 1974 and is based on the constitution of the country, which calls for the consideration of children as a group with special needs that should be prioritised and protected. Although the policy document does not explicitly mention rights, it can be considered a rights-based policy, as it is based on the constitution, which emphasises fundamental rights including the right to food and education.

In 1994, the Department of Women and Child Development, in the Ministry of Health and Family Welfare, brought out a document that aimed to highlight the rights of children. This document describes the sequences of international events that led to the UNCRC and India's ratification of it. It attempts to place the ongoing child development programs in India into a child rights perspective; however, it does not clearly acknowledge participation rights or their importance and presence in ongoing programs for children.

In 1997, the Government of India prepared another document, which attempted to review the existing child programs in light of the rights perspective and called for a review of legislation for children. However, this document also omits explicit reference to participation rights. In 2000, a group of experts formulated a report indicating what each right means in

India, how to operationalise the rights, and the strategies needed to ensure that child rights are implemented. In 2001, the National Commission for Children was formed and called for the formation of state level commissions. The major aim of the Commission is to improve the situation of children across the country through ensuring child rights in all parts of the nation.

The study

India is widely known for its vast social, cultural and economic diversity. The study in India initially undertook a review of the existing literature from a variety of sources with a view to documenting the perspectives existing in the various published and unpublished materials. Based on this understanding, a primary research project was undertaken. The objective of this research was to understand the meanings of child participation, the forms of child participation, and the differentials according to the age, gender, place of residence and educational status of children. An attempt was also made to identify the factors that limit or promote child participation in diverse social and cultural milieux.

Methodology

As noted earlier, the study began with a review of literature on child participation as it has evolved through changing social and cultural contexts. This review helped us to understand the historical contexts and also to appreciate some of the attempts aimed at promoting child participation in India. Using the broad paradigm of qualitative research, the study used a variety of methods to capture diverse perspectives of child participation from the stakeholders, who included children, parents, community leaders, representatives from NGOs working with children, lawyers, government personnel and academicians. During one of the study group meetings organised in 2005, a one day workshop on child participation was also conducted with eight international participants and 28 participants from India, representing a range of stakeholder groups and geographical diversity. In addition to providing an opportunity for interface between national and international individuals engaged in research and advocacy activities on child participation, this workshop was also viewed as an avenue to bring together stakeholders from various parts of India, thus enabling us to obtain diverse perspectives on the concept of child participation.

This workshop was followed by a one day Children's Meet, in which about 35 children from Mumbai representing varied social, cultural and economic backgrounds participated. Children were divided into four groups according to age and gender. Facilitators moderated group discussions on various aspects of child participation with a view to eliciting children's perspectives. Subsequently, key informant interviews were conducted with representatives from other stakeholder groups such as community leaders, parents, academicians, and NGO functionaries. Overall, we conducted 20 key informant interviews with adult stakeholders and seven focus group discussions (FGDs) with children. Of the seven FGDs with children, four were conducted during the Children's Meet and the remaining three were conducted in other settings (school and community settings).

Meanings and definitions of child participation

The primary research for this study was carried out in Mumbai; data was obtained through a national level workshop, a Children's Meet, key informant interviews and focus group discussions. During the workshop on child participation held in February 2005, the participants were divided into various groups; the mandate of one of the groups was to discuss the meaning of child participation. This group consisted of representatives from three spheres: NGOs, government, and academia. All of the members of this group were from India. The group felt that children could be responsible and decide things in groups; they believed that children over the age of six were capable of making decisions. They also believed that children were able take on responsibilities at home and could help parents, but that a long-term campaign was necessary to enhance children's participation at the family level. The group also suggested that vulnerable groups and children from middle and upper class families should be treated separately when analysing the meaning, levels, and spheres of child participation. Finally, they recommended that age-specific developmental maturities also be taken into consideration.

After detailed discussion, the group arrived at three alternative definitions of the concept of child participation. The definitions were:

Definition1: *Child participation is a process and a condition of creating an environment where a child expresses his/her own needs and which involves decision making, contribution and evaluation of the same for further improvement which concerns their life and well-being.*

Definition2: *Construction of child participation evolves with social, psychological, mental, physical, emotional and an integrated involvement in the decision making, keeping in mind regional and cultural contexts and age specific needs and capacities of the child.*

Definition3: *Child participation is enabling the child to involve him/herself in areas which are appropriate to the age and maturity of the child and which will contribute to the overall development in all areas for his/her optimum development and welfare and which would help in the development of positive self-concept and self-esteem.*

The general agreement was that, at each stage, the child should be encouraged to develop independent and logical thinking, reasoning, decision making and problem solving by giving them an environment conducive to doing so. In general, the adults vehemently agreed that child participation is essential for the overall development of children and would also help to cultivate in them a responsibility towards society. One representative from an NGO known for its activities promoting the involvement of children said that *'Having dialogues with children and respecting their point of view play a crucial role in child participation'*. Similarly, another representative said *'children should be responsible not only for areas concerning them, but for the community as a whole'*.

These viewpoints on child participation emerged from group discussions; however, the experiences from the individual interviews with key informants and from the focus group discussions with children provided us with a slightly different perspective, indicating that the understanding of the concept of participation varies across stakeholder groups and even within particular stakeholder groups. As a group, the adult stakeholders were able to better conceptualise what child participation may mean and to identify its various forms. Key informant interviews, however, showed that the individual understanding of the term is more limited and often restricted to the sphere(s) in which the individual is currently working. Some of the perspectives from the key informant interviews regarding what is meant by child participation can be seen in Table 1.

Table 1: Meaning of 'child participation', from key informant interviews

1	Children cannot participate because they are small.
2	Opportunity to express what they (children) think.
3	Not able to say, as we do not know what is meant by child.
4	Participation in education, the components being enrolment, attendance, course completion; varies according to age category.
5	Allowing the child to speak.
6	Meaning of child participation depends upon adults' perception about child's involvement in decision making.
7	Participation meaning the proper guidance and control.
8	Children taking part in the decision making of the institution (in the institutional setup).
9	Engagement of children in studies, or in games, or in work.
10	Making the best use of whatever resources that are being given in the institution (in the institutional setup). The child has to search and try out for his goal or something that he wants to achieve in life with the help of inputs that we give in our organisation.
11	Participation of the child in the family.
12	Participation in cultural programs and festivals.
13	The idea of participation means taking the responsibility for your own behaviour.
14	The process of exercising one's own choice.
15	If children do not participate in employment, many families would be starving. Thus it is very difficult to say what participation means. Unless there is some clarity on who this child is and what is meant by participation either with regard to their own life decisions or regard to their family's economic activity or larger issues, politics, or economy, it is difficult to say what participation means.
16	Empowerment of children.

It is clear that child participation is viewed and understood differently even by educated adults. That such meanings range from the view that 'children should not participate' to 'child participation means empowerment' tells us the extent of the confusion regarding the concept amongst adults; the very people who we are counting on to be instrumental in enhancing child participation rights. The confusion among adults cannot be more clearly seen than from the observation that we are still not sure who is a child, what is meant by 'child' and what the spheres of participation are that we should be concerned about.

The Children's Meet gave us yet another range of meanings of the term 'child participation'. For some of the children, participation means 'going to school', 'going for tuition', or 'going with friends to buy gifts'. For others, child participation means 'freedom of expression', 'to be involved in everything', 'to win' or 'to play in groups'. It should be noted here that the children who participated in the meet were from different socio-economic backgrounds, including those living in slum areas of Mumbai and those living in wealthy residential locations. Also, the extent and type of exposure to participation these children experienced was different in the sense that the group included children growing up in controlled atmospheres (where parental control was high and exposure was limited to school), as well as children with a high level of exposure gained through NGO activities. The researchers made no attempt to delineate children according to socio-economic background or the extent of exposure. It was observed that the broadness of the concept of child participation varied, particularly according to the extent of exposure a child had experienced.

Socio-economic and cultural differentials in child participation

Differentials in living conditions, lifestyles and access to resources exist in all societies; therefore, one should also expect differences in child participation across population groups. This is particularly relevant to nations like India, where the diversities are not only geographical but are marked in terms of the existing social, cultural and economic status, even within smaller geographical boundaries. For this reason, the present study sought to identify the major aspects that contribute to the variations in the extent and forms of child participation. The workshop on child participation kept this issue fairly open-ended, therefore giving space to the participants to identify various factors contributing to the differentials. However, in the key informant interviews and the focus group discussions with children, we limited the guidelines to selected aspects; these aspects were identified based on our understanding of Indian society and also on the major determining factors that consistently arose during earlier study group meetings and during the one day workshop, where one of the groups focused only on this topic.

The group that discussed the issues of social and cultural differences in child participation tended to differentiate between 'positive participation' and 'negative participation'. This was due to a perceived need to give differential treatment to the concept of child participation when dealing with 'tribals' and 'non-tribals', as the cultural and traditional practices are vastly different. Likewise, the group believed that the family background, the location where a child is born (rural or urban), and the educational status of their parents significantly influence child participation and thus contribute to the differentials.

The general opinion expressed was that children growing up in urban areas are more exposed to opportunities for participation and are also exposed to media, which is a source of motivation for children to participate. In contrast, rural children are tightly bonded to their families and communities and have opportunities for participation only as a part of larger groups. In general, rural girls have much fewer avenues to participate, not only compared to rural boys, but also compared to their counterparts in urban areas.

Table 2: Gender differences in child participation: salient views of key informants

1.	There will not be any gender difference because girls are in no way inferior in terms of making decisions or participating.
2.	Gender plays a large role in participation. The girl child is given fewer opportunities. Equal opportunity must be given to boys and girls to participate.
3.	In a patriarchal society like India, boys are given important roles so that they become bold and courageous. But even they are not given enough participation opportunities.
4.	There will be differences in decision making between a male child and a female child. Girl children may decide about kitchen utensils and boys may decide about buying appliances.
5.	Male children are given a lot more freedom because ultimately male children have to become bread earners. Secondly, the sexuality of the girl has to be protected, therefore her movements are controlled. There is a belief that girl children cannot do certain things as they are meant for boys. The entire socialisation process, which segregates boys and girls, orients them into different directions.
6.	There are fewer opportunities for females. Girl children can have a greater say in domestic matters, picking up domestic skills, but not so much with regard to their studies or their career.
7.	The problems of boys and girls differ; so levels of participation also differ. Girls are restricted from making decisions.
8.	If a male child is the elder one, they take the decision. If a girl child is the elder one, parents will ask her to learn domestic work as after sometime she would get married. Parents want the girl to stay home. In Mumbai city also this is happening. Only rarely there is participation even in educated families.
9.	In Muslim communities there is no participation of girls. There is more participation for boys.
10.	Even in educated families, girls do not have a say. In choosing a husband also there is no chance to express their desire.

11.	Even in city as in rural areas, the male is pampered. The girl child has to work, even if she wants to go to school.
12.	There may be some gender differences in some families.
13.	Daughters get better opportunities.
14.	Sometimes it will be our son's chance to speak up, sometimes our daughter's. Gender differences are never felt.
15.	There are opportunities for both our children. The only thing is that our daughter decides her own things and our boy is not like that. There can be a difference in how they utilise the opportunities.

As can be observed from Table 2, the views expressed by key informants cover a wide spectrum of understanding about the issue of participation. Some parents (who mainly resided in Mumbai and were from middle-class families) felt that there was no gender difference in relation to participation, and even if there was, it was in favor of females. Yet, a majority of key informants of this study held that there are gender differences, and that girls are given fewer opportunities in both rural and urban areas. The following quote from one of the interviews summarises this general opinion:

> *Gender will not make any difference in participation, if left to the individual child. Whether it's a girl or a boy, either can decide what they want. The issue of gender comes because of the social way in which you look at the girl child or the boy child. So like socially speaking we say that boys can make so many decisions and we do not allow girls to make so many decisions. In the Indian culture from the beginning we say that if girls start making decisions, afterwards it will be very difficult for them when they go to another house. For boys we say, boys will have to support a family. Thus, they must make their own decisions so that they will become independent. We always feel that girls should be made timid and dependent so as to dissuade girls from making similar levels of mental and cognitive ability.*

While acknowledging the prevalence of gender differences in a patriarchal society, the key informants by and large felt that there should be equal opportunities given to both boys and girls. However, they cautioned that as the needs of boys and girls are different, treating boys and girls the same without considering their needs would not be the right approach in bringing out gender equality in child participation.

Interestingly, most key informants did not mention either the presence or absence of differentials in child participation arising because of religion. Whether one can take this as an indication of the absence of differentials is not clear, as the question put forward to them included both religion and caste. More probable is the fact that caste differences are much more prominent than differences based on religion. Differences between scheduled castes or tribes and non-scheduled castes were highlighted by several of the key informants. Some key informants felt that as avenues for education are fewer for lower caste children, they would not be aware of participation. While this view highlights caste differences, it also suggests that 'participation' should necessarily be linked to education, or at least opportunities for education. However, other key informants believed that it is not necessarily true that children from lower educational strata do not participate. They suggested that it was possible that children from lower caste groups may in fact have a little more freedom than those from higher caste or class groups, as parents in these groups often hold a much more protective attitude towards their children, resulting in greater control.

The general opinion was that class affiliation can have an influence on the extent of children's participation. This was perceived to be due to the dominance of the rich and upper caste groups in society: *'Class barriers prevent children from having exposure. How many children in Chembur (Mumbai) who are from the middle and upper class mingle with the children from low income families?'* At the same time, it was also suggested that children from lower economic strata may have more freedom, as the extent of family control is often much lower. However, the importance of money in opening up opportunities for participation was still highlighted, with one key informant observing: *'If you do not have the money you cannot go for any activities even if you like to, like dramatics, coaching classes, music classes etc.'.* Therefore, a lack of money may limit children's opportunities to get to know other children.

Opportunities for child participation in everyday life

Overall, the stakeholder groups believed that opportunities for children to participate do exist, but are limited and constrained by the existing social, economic and cultural contexts. The spheres of child participation identified by the stakeholders were generally limited to education, home and family, and work. The stakeholders only rarely mentioned other opportunities, and by and large were not able to identify specific avenues for child participation, with many of the opinions remaining vague. The exceptions to this general trend were those participants who are currently engaged in child participation activities and those who are engaged in child research.

Children themselves expressed their opinions about the opportunities for them to participate in four spheres of their life: home, school, religious spaces and society. They felt that at home they participated by helping other family members, especially their mother, or by taking care of younger siblings. Some of the children expressed a broader role for children in the family, such as *'to participate in all decisions of the family'*, *'to know our duties and fulfill them'*, *'to take part in every matter of concern in the family'* or *'knowing your responsibility, divide and share the responsibility at home'*. Thus, the questions on opportunities for participation elicited responses not only on that aspect, but also on the likely level and nature of participation.

School is a sphere where children are expected to become involved in many activities. But for many children, school is not a comfortable place that promotes child participation. While some of the children said they took part in 'every activity', others felt 'not free in the school', or said they 'feel scared', had a 'lack of confidence', or that the 'teacher shouts', and the 'teacher cares for only those who study well'. This suggests that opportunities for children to participate are skewed and mostly available to those who are smart and display good academic performance. At home, the extent of opportunities varied primarily according to the attitude of parents and the capacity of children to make use of the existing opportunities. As evident from the discussions with the children, and also with the key informants, avenues for participation may also depend upon the educational and economic status of parents. While parents who participated in the study reiterated that they provided 'sufficient' opportunities for the child, other key informants felt that even in educated families there are many restrictions on children's participation in family matters. Most of the children felt that there were some opportunities for them to participate in religious activities; most of these opportunities related to taking part in festivals and other celebrations, which helped them to gain more self-confidence and to make new friends.

The key informants who participated in the study also believed that limited opportunities exist for children to participate. They suggested that the extent of opportunities and the level of participation were determined by the child's age, gender and place of residence, and whether or not the child was in the educational system. While many key informants felt that parents limit children's participation, some opined that parents, compelled by a felt need to excel in a competitive world, push their children to participate in everything. However, such participation is generally aimed at acquiring new skills and taking part in competitions that provide an avenue for the child to express themselves.

In some instances, schools also encourage children's participation beyond their traditional involvement in annual days or sport activities. For instance, one of the teachers who took part in the study stated:

'Because we have separated the world of adults and children so strongly, when we talk of child participation we have to very consciously think of certain mechanisms we have to put things in place in which children can come and participate. For example, in schools we have student councils or we have student committees. The child-to-child health program is a very useful example in which you can teach older children messages which they will pass on to the younger children.'

Some of the institutions that provide shelter to children separated from their parents also provide opportunities for children to participate, though to a limited extent:

'Actually in our programs we involve them [children] from the beginning. For example, when we have annual functions, they are the ones who perform in front of guests, sponsors and donors. Actually the motive of our organisation, the goal that we perceive for our organisation, is that somewhere along the line these ex-students will take over the organisation.'

The present study revealed that middle-class parents appear to promote the participation of children in family matters. This was evident from their account of the opportunities they give their children:

'In my family we make them involved in important decision making activities like financial activities and buying some important articles at home. When the children were small we did not involve them in important matters. But when they had grown up, we gave them that freedom. Nowadays if the children have to attend some

function, they come late. We have trust in them and allow them to come at that time. Here also we tell them to come before a certain time.'

'They participate in almost all the things in the family. But they don't take part in big decisions of the family. They discuss with us activities in school.'

These examples suggest that, in addition to the socio-cultural factors mentioned as determinants of opportunities, the aspects of 'compulsory' and 'voluntary' also have an impact on child participation. It appears that if child participation is voluntary and left to the child, then avenues for participation are limited. In other words, it is the responsibility of adults to create opportunities for child participation and to gently persuade children to get involved.

Conclusion

This study began with the assumption, based on our understanding of Indian society, that there could be differentials in the understanding of the concept and in the extent of child participation. That the concept of child participation is understood differently across stakeholder groups, and even within particular stakeholder groups, points to the importance of designing advocacy activities that clearly define the terms 'participation' and 'child participation', and that identify the salient areas where children's participation should be encouraged. The study found that there is a range of meanings attached to the term 'participation', ranging from 'complete non-involvement' to 'complete involvement' in decision making processes. While this is in line with the ladder suggested by UNICEF, observations from this study suggest that the level of participation depends upon the spheres of participation, the maturity of individual children, and the perceived social roles of children by age, gender, education and work status.

The study confirmed the hypothesis of social, cultural and economic differentials in the levels of child participation and helped to identify the salient factors that contribute to such differences. The most important variables in the Indian context as revealed by the present exercise are gender and caste-class affiliations. The patriarchal nature of Indian society, the different opportunities available, and the indifferent attitude towards those hailing from lower socio-economic strata can limit children from participating at all, let alone participating effectively. Whether the child is a student or not is also an important determinant of their participation. However, in this case (whether the child is a student or non-student), instead of defining the limits of participation, the affiliation (or non-affiliation) decides the spheres or avenues of the child's participation. Finally, it is also generally perceived that children from urban areas have more opportunities to express themselves and to become involved in various activities when compared to their counterparts in rural areas.

Following the major social and cultural barriers to participation, the key informants in this study felt that parents (not all adults, as it is often held) are primarily responsible for the limited participation of children. This means that in the existing scenario of socio-cultural differences across population groups, if child participation is to be improved, parents should be seen as the most important stakeholders. Advocacy activities or program initiatives that do not involve parents are unlikely to have much chance of sustained success.

Lastly, a discussion of the methodological approach to researching child participation is required. The present study tried to use some of the widely used methods in an innovative way. Using workshops to elicit insights into a particular phenomenon is not at all new. In this research, the workshop on child participation served two purposes; one not directly related to the research, and one having a direct bearing. This workshop provided a platform for those working on child participation to interact and share experiences and perspectives. More importantly, it provided us with a collective understanding of the concept and process of child participation in the Indian context and thus helped immensely in designing the further course of the research.

The use of a 'Children's Meet' as an avenue for gathering information from children worked effectively for this study. Through providing an opportunity for children from different socio-economic backgrounds to mingle and express, it proved an excellent platform for the discussion of issues of child participation. Children were very enthusiastic to share their concerns and to discuss participation issues in groups. However, the mixing of children from varying backgrounds had its limitations; initially, children living in slum areas were not forthcoming as they felt somewhat inferior in front of their more elite counterparts who had access to better clothing and were attending better schools. Once the initial inhibition faded however, the atmosphere became much more conducive to free interaction and expression. From the experience of the 'Children's Meet', we also learnt that it is not the socio-economic background alone, but the exposure of children that makes a difference in child participation.

Acknowledgments

We are grateful to the Board of Research Studies, Tata Institute of Social Sciences, Mumbai, India for sponsoring the research in India. The activities of the Asia-Pacific study group on child participation were actively facilitated by Childwatch International, Oslo, Norway.

References

Bajpai, Asha 2004, *Child rights in India: law, policy and practice,* Oxford University Press, New Delhi.

Black, Maggie 2003, *Opening minds, opening opportunities: children's participation in action for working children,* Save the Children, London.

Cussianovich, Alejandro and Maria A Marquez 2002, *Towards a protagonist participation of boys, girls and teenagers,* Save the Children Regional Office Sweden, Lima.

Flekkøy, G Malfrid and Kaufman, Natalie H 1997, *The participation rights of the child: rights and responsibilities in family and society*, Children in Charge Series 4, Jessica Kingsley Publishers.

Franklin, Bob (ed.) 2005, *The new handbook of children's rights,* Routledge, London.

Government of India 1994, *Universal Children's Day,* Department of Women & Child Development, Ministry of Human Resource Development, Govt. of India, New Delhi.

Government of India 1997, *Convention on the Rights of the Child, Country Report,* Ministry of Human Resource Development, Dept. of Women and Child Development, New Delhi.

Hart, Roger A 1992, *Children's participation: from tokenism to citizenship,* UNICEF Innocenti Research Centre, Florence.

Hodgkin, Rachel and Newell, Peter 2002, *Implementation handbook for the Convention on the Rights of the Child: fully revised edition*, UNICEF, New York.

Kaufman, N. & Rizzini, I (eds.) 2002, *Globalisation and children: exploring potentials for enhancing opportunities in the lives of children and youth*, Kluwer Academic/Plennum Publishers.

Lansdown, Gerison 2001, *Promoting children's participation in democratic decision making,* UNICEF Innocenti Research Centre, Florence.

Miller, Judy 2003, *Never too young: how young people can take responsibility and make decisions,* Save the Children, UK, London.

Nandkarni, MV 2006, *Hinduism: a Gandhian perspective,* Ane books India, New Delhi.

Premi, MK 2002, 'The girl child: some issues for consideration', *paper presented in symposium on sex ratio in India,* IIPS Mumbai, 10–11 January.

Rajani, Rakesh (ed.) 2000, *The political participation of children,* Harvard Center for Population and Development Studies, Cambridge, MA.

Rajani, Rakesh 2001, *The participation rights of adolescents: a strategic approach,* UNICEF, New York.

Reddy, Nandana and Ratna, Kavita 2002, *A journey in children's participation,* Concerned for Working Children (CWC), Bangalore, India.

Shier, Harry 2001, 'Pathways to participation: openings, opportunities and obligations', *Children and society*, vol. 15, no. 2, pp. 107–117.

Theis, Joachim 2001, *Defining child and youth participation,* UNICEF EAPRO, Bangkok.

UNICEF 2001, *The participation rights of adolescents: a strategic approach*, Working Paper Series, Programme Division, New York, NY, USA.

UNICEF 2002, *The state of the world's children 2003: issue on participation,* UNICEF, New York.

UNICEF 2001, *The state of the world's children: early childhood,* UNICEF.

Chapter 4
Thailand

Nittaya J. Kotchabhadi, Dalapat Yossatorn, Athiwat Plengsa-ard
and Nithivadee Noochaiya

Introduction

Thailand is situated in the heart of the Southeast Asia mainland. The country covers an area of 513,115 km2 and extends about 1,620 kilometers from north to south and 775 kilometres from east to west. In 2004, the population of Thailand was approximately 63.7 million people, of whom 49.5 % were males and 50.5% were females. Almost 69% of the population lives in rural areas, with the remaining 31% living in urban centers (6.7 million people live in Bangkok alone).

While the population has doubled over the last 30 years, this was largely due to strong population growth throughout the 1970s. During the 1980s, however, population growth halted abruptly—as a result, the ratio of children under 15 years in the population has fallen dramatically, from 38.5% in 1960 to 29.2% in 1990. The population growth rate is currently around 1.5% per annum, while the average total fertility rate (total live births per woman surviving the childbearing years) is just under the replacement level of two (1.8). Therefore, the proportion of the population in each age group up to 40 is expected to level out and there will be a slight reduction in the number of children aged between 10 and 18 (UNDP 2006).

Thailand's Ninth National Economic and Social Development Plan (2002–2006) focused on the balanced development of human, social, economic and environmental resources. Thailand's development vision for the next 20 years focuses on the alleviation of poverty and the upgrading of the quality of life for Thai people, so that "sustainable development and well-being for all can be achieved".

Health

Thailand has traditionally focused on preventive public health measures such as sanitation, clean water supplies and vaccinations as the most cost-effective means of improving the general health status of the population. Today, primary healthcare and universal healthcare have improved child health status remarkably, resulting in reduced infant and child mortality rates, reduced malnutrition, and immunisation coverage of more than 90% of Thai children.

The "30 baht health care scheme", which offers hospital treatment at just 30 baht per visit, has been critical in ensuring access to health care for the poor. It represents an historic step in creating a safety net for millions of people not employed by the civil service or private sector. However, no analysis of the impacts of the scheme on child health or family investment in children has yet been conducted in Thailand.

Education

In recent years, there has been increased emphasis on education. In the 2002 academic year, the total number of students was more than 14 million. In 2002, the average number of years that a person had attended school was 7.8 (for persons aged over 15 years); an increase from an average of 6.9 years in 1996. Over 68% of all young people aged between 12 and 17 are enrolled in secondary schools, although research has shown that girls tend to drop out of school up to a year before boys. According to the UNDP 2003 Human Development Report for Thailand, girls in 11 provinces are less likely to be in secondary school than males of the same age.

At present, education reform is one of the priorities among government policies. The 1997 Constitution and the *National Educational Act* can be seen as principles and guidelines for the provision and development of Thai education, aiming to prepare Thai people for a learning society in a knowledge-based economy.

However, investments in basic education, while impressive in the numbers of children they have reached, have not produced significantly positive learning outcomes for the general population. The *National Education Act B.E. 2542* (1999) and Amendments (*Second National Education Act B.E. 2545*) (2002) have a clear focus on developing humans, families, and children. Emphasis on collaboration by all stake-holders is now widespread. Initiatives include the participation and the involvement of parents, communities, teachers and children; the provision of good care for early childhood; improving the quality of education at all levels; extending basic education to all school-age children; moving from six to nine years of compulsory schooling and working towards further extension to 12 years; and providing continuous training for teachers.

The status of child participation in Thailand

Across the world, child participation is an essential element of society. All children have rights to speak out, take part in making decisions and participate in families, schools and community activities. However, in the real world, some children do not inherit their right to a childhood of love, care and protection in a family and community environment (UNICEF 2005). Children whose rights to safety and dignity are denied are also impoverished. Each year, tens of millions of children are the victims of exploitation, violence and abuse, which rob them of their childhood, preventing them from achieving anything close to their full potential (UNICEF 2007). Children may also suffer from neglect when both parents must work, or when rapid economic and social changes prevent parents from giving sufficient time or attention to their children.

In 2002, Thailand's National Economic and Social Development Committee suggested that interaction within Thai families had declined and interactions between family, community and society had also decreased (The National Economic and Social Development Committee 2004).

Thai children experience problems both within the family and the community because of the rapid change in technology, economics, social values and life in general. The Ministry of Social Development and Human Security (2004) reported that problems experienced by young people include the first sexual encounter (for children between 13 and 19 years old), HIV/AIDS (for young people under 25 years of age), criminal/deviant behavior (e.g. robbery, drug abuse and violence), suicide, psychosis and physical abuse.

Despite these issues, a majority of Thai children are sincerely looked after and cared for by parents and family. However, the Thai tradition concerning "respect" for seniority and the hierarchical code does pose some problems. "Children should be seen but not heard" is a common expression in Thai society, while "good children" are those that are obedient and grateful. As such, children's basic right of participation, especially in terms of assertiveness and decision making, is often in conflict with the expectations of conservative adults.

Children's participation has been considered on many occasions in Thailand, including:
- The Convention on the Rights of the Child in Thailand (1992): the rights of survival, the rights of protection, the rights of development and the rights of participation

- The Child's Rights by the Constitution of the Kingdom of Thailand (1997): child, youth and individuals in the family having rights to receive the protection of the state from violence and injustice
- The Eight and Ninth National Economic and Social Development Plan (1997–2001), (2002–2006): human development is an essential factor and the center of learning includes all elements of society
- Child rights by the *National Education Act B.E. 2542* (1999): in the provision of education, all individuals shall have equal rights and opportunities to receive basic education provided by the state for the duration of at least 12 years. Such education shall be provided universally, shall be of quality and free of charge
- The *Act of Parliament on Child Protection* (2003): to work together to take care, protect and support the child by having a support system, child protection and a security system. Promote responsible action by the family, community, and professionals, including the role of the state and private sector working together for the protection of the child.

Methodology

The Thai research project included both a qualitative and a quantitative study.

Qualitative study

The qualitative study involved 58 children, 20 parents, 15 teachers, 10 community leaders and five policy makers in Mahasawat Subdistrict and Salaya district, Nakhon Pathom Province, and was conducted between October and December 2004. Children were separated into the following groups: male/female, 12–14 years old/15–17 years old, urban/rural. Documentary analysis, questionnaires, focus group discussions and in-depth interviews were used as follows:

1. Documentary analysis: legislation, policy, reports, instances of participation—formal and informal
2. Questionnaire about the details of participation action for the children and parents
3. Focus group discussions:
   - Eight groups of children (12–14 and 15–17 years old, male and female, urban and rural)
   - Parents in urban and rural locations
   - Teachers in urban schools and rural schools

4. In-depth interviews:
   - Community leaders in urban and rural locations

　∘　Community policy makers

Quantitative study

A two-state stratified sampling method was used for selecting 1,670 house-holds from five provinces. Each province represented one of the five geographic regions of Thailand. Adolescents between 12 and 18 years old, living in the selected households, were surveyed by self-administered questionnaire.

Findings

Analysis of the data collected during both the qualitative and quantitative studies revealed five key themes:
1. Definitions of children's participation
2. Opportunities available for children to participate
3. Differences in children's participation due to gender, age and socio-economic factors
4. Influences on and barriers to children's participation
5. Benefits of children's participation

Interestingly, there was no significant difference between the definitions of children's participation provided by adults and those provided by children themselves. Both adults and children understood participation to mean children having access to information, being able to express themselves, to take part in activities and to make decisions about issues affecting them.

Despite this understanding, few children specifically identified being involved in decision making as an activity in which they participated. Instead, they nominated domestic chores and family, creative, religious, and cultural activities as those areas in which they most often participated. Further documentary analysis revealed that children were most likely to participate in formal group activities, such as those organised through schools, religious institutions and structured community organisations. Informal participation was found to be primarily focused on helping within the home by doing chores or caring for other family members.

Differences were found in the nature and level of children's participation according to age, gender and socio-economic status. In general, girls participated more in the home than boys, particularly as they became older. While participating in informal activities, younger children were found to be less likely than older children to participate in organised activities, such as sporting teams or school-based activities. Children from lower socio-economic communities (which were predominantly rural

43

communities) also had fewer opportunities to participate in organised activities.

The attitude of adults, particularly parents, was found to be an important factor in the nature and level of children's participation. The research revealed that Thai adults generally take a positive attitude towards children's participation in organised activities, although attitudes about children participating in decision making were less clear. Furthermore, the willingness and ability of individual children also strongly influenced their participation levels and the types of activities that they took part in.

Finally, the social and developmental benefits of children's participation were revealed through an analysis of previous case studies, which demonstrated how children's participation assists in the physical, cognitive and social development of the child, while also contributing to the strengthening of family and community relations.

Definitions of children's participation

The documentary analysis highlighted some broad understandings of child participation. These included: 1) children should participate in all matters concerning them, their learning and their development; 2) opportunities should be given to children of all ages ranging from new-born to infant to late teens; and 3) opportunities created should not be restricted to areas of expression or ideas—participation should cover many other activities that will allow children to grow physically, mentally, intellectually, socially, emotionally and spiritually.

The children and adults who participated in the Thailand study provided a range of understandings about children's participation. Definitions included children having access to information, children being able to express themselves, children making decisions about issues affecting them and children taking part in activities. While these definitions varied, the responses provided were similar across both children and adults.

Opportunities available for children to participate

Children identified a range of ways in which they were able to participate. These included undertaking household chores (92.3%), being involved in family issues (76.0%), creative activities (74.3%), religious activities (73.7%), cultural activities (68.9%), taking care of family members (66.8%), sharing their opinions and exchanging information (62.7%) and earning an income (51.4%). Being involved in decision making was not explicitly identified.

The quantitative study found that many opportunities for children to participate were provided in formal settings and were primarily group-focused. In particular, schools provided many opportunities for children to participate, with 88.9% of children participating in some form of school-related activity. Almost half (47.8%) of the children also participated in group activities organised by religious institutions, while 42.4% participated in formal group activities in the community, such as the Scouting movement.

The documentary analysis also primarily focused on formal participatory opportunities. For example, Kangsadaporn (2004) discussed the participation of junior high school students in developing drug prevention measures in schools. The case study undertaken at Rongrien Kayai Okat School revealed that the students were keen to be involved in the design of the program and had previously participated in similar activities organised by the school.

Differences in children's participation due to gender, age and socio-economic factors

The research found that the nature and level of children's participation varies significantly with age, gender, and socio-economic status. For example, a community-based participatory research project conducted in Salaya found that girls spent more time at home than boys, either watching television or undertaking domestic chores (Yossatorn, Vorakitphokatorn & Kotchabhakdi 2002). The research also found that younger children of both genders, while regularly participating in informal activities, were less likely to participate in organised activities, such as sports, which were primarily undertaken by older boys. Older girls were more likely to participate in domestic chores than either boys or younger girls.

The study also found that children from low-income communities (which were predominantly rural communities) were less likely to participate in organised activities, suggesting a correlation between socio-economic status and the level and nature of children's participation.

A difference in the nature and level of participation between boys and girls was also revealed through the quantitative study. Only 30.9% of children thought that there was no difference in the way each gender participated in school activities, with only 30.7% and 30.1% respectively believing there was also no difference in the way boys and girls participated in religious activities or home activities. The remaining 70% of children believed there were some differences in the way each gender participated.

Influences on and barriers to children's participation

The Thailand study highlighted the important role that adults play in facilitating children's participation. Over half of the children (50.3%) stated that adults, especially parents, have a significant influence over the nature and level of children's participation. In particular, children expressed a desire for adult acceptance of their views and support for their activities. Pleasingly, the research found that adults' influence over children's participation was generally positive, with only 16.3% of children stating that adults were an obstacle to participation. This suggests that most adults encourage children to participate and that non-participation may be due to other factors.

The nature and level of children's participation was also found to be influenced by the willingness of the individual child and how interesting they found a particular activity. Over 47% of children believed they themselves were a significant factor in how and where they participated, with 27.3% describing themselves as an obstacle to participation, due to inadequate skills, abilities or initiative to participate in a given activity. Likewise, the nature of a given activity was found to have an impact on children's participation, with 23.7% of children stating that their participation depended on the situation or activity involved. Over half of the children (50.3%) also identified certain activities as obstacles to their participation, suggesting that there are particular activities that children are unable (socially, culturally or physically) to participate in, despite their willingness to do so.

Despite these barriers to participation, the research found that almost 79% of children were satisfied with the level and nature of their participation.

Benefits of children's participation

The social and developmental benefits of children's participation were primarily revealed through the documentary analysis. Two case studies are presented below, highlighting how children's participation has been found to contribute to greater co-operation and stronger family/community functioning, as well as to the social development of the children themselves.

A study into a school-run program for children at risk of contracting HIV/AIDS (UNICEF 2003) revealed some interesting benefits of children's participation. The program involved both parents and children, and encouraged children to identify new activities for their school. After participating in the program, the children reported feeling closer to their parents and having greater respect for the opinions of others. Over 95% of the study participants reflected that the participatory experience had strengthened relationships within the family. The children were found to have become better listeners and were more confident about expressing their ideas and concerns. They were also more willing to take on responsibilities at home as they felt that their parents now had more respect for their opinions and abilities.

A community-based child development project in Mahasawat Subdistrict (Yossatorn, Plengsa-ard, Noochaiya & Kotchabhakdi 2004) revealed similar benefits. Observations made during the program were combined with data collected through surveys of children, parents, program organisers and community leaders, both prior to and following the program. The results showed that most respondents believed that participation in the program had improved children's physical, cognitive, social and moral wellbeing. Specifically, the children reported that they had learned more about specific occupations, co-operation with other children, and physical fitness.

Conclusion and limitations

Children in Thailand today are afforded greater opportunities to particip- ate than ever before, particularly in terms of organised educational, reli- gious and cultural activities. A widespread recognition of the benefits and importance of children's participation appears to exist, although its integ- ration into everyday life continues to be hampered by traditional construc- tions of children's place in the family and social hierarchy. Therefore, des- pite commonalities in the way children and adults define children's parti- cipation, in practice, children's participation is often focused more on formal organised activities, rather than on decision making that will affect children in the long term. This is especially so in the home, where chil- dren's participation is primarily limited to domestic chores, and opportun- ities for involvement in decision making are few.

Adults therefore have a crucial part to play in improving the status of children's participation in Thailand. While the research found that many adults view children's participation favorably, more can be done to ensure that adults understand the benefits to be achieved by children participating in a wider range of activities, including the decision making process. Like- wise, the study revealed a need to educate children on the importance of participation, both for their individual personal development and for sup- porting and growing community and social relations in the future. Children also need to be made more aware of their rights in terms of participation, while being encouraged to take on responsibilities (with assistance where appropriate) that will help them to develop the skills, abilities and attitudes that will enable them to positively influence their families and communities.

References

Kangsadaporn, Angkana 2004, 'Participation of junior high school students in developing drug prevention in school: the case study on Ron- grien Kayai Okat schools, under the jurisdiction of Bangkok Met- ropolitan Administration', Thesis in Master Degree of Social Ad- ministration, Bangkok:Thammasat University.
National Youth Bureau, Office of the Prime Minister and UNICEF, Chil- dren in Thailand 1990–2000: country report on the follow up to the World Summit for Children.
NESDB 2005, 'Social outlook 2005', *Social issue report*, vol. 3 no. 4, December.

Office of the Education Council, Ministry of Education, National Education Act B.E.2542 (1999) and Amendments (Second National Education Act B.E.2545 (2002)).

The National Economic and Social Development Committee 2004, *The strategy framework on integrate the family development*, The National Economic and Social Development Committee, Bangkok.

UNDP 2003, Human Development Report, United Nations Development Programme.

UNDP 2006, Human Development Report, United Nations Development Programme, http://hdr.undp.org/hdr2006/statistics/ (accessed 16th October 2009)

UNICEF 2003, The state of the world's children. http://www.unicef.org/sowc03/ (accessed 16th October 2009)

UNICEF 2005, Children and young people in Thailand: UNICEF Situation Analysis.

UNICEF 2007, The state of the world's children.

Yossatorn, Vorakitphokatorn & Kotchabhakdi 2002, Ninth International Congress of Behavioral Medicine Sofitel Central Plaza Hotel, Bangkok, Thailand 2006 : Bridging Behavior and Health – Connecting the Hemispheres National Institute for Child and Family Development, Mahidol University

Yossatorn Dalapat, Athiwat Plengsa-ard, Nithivadee Noochaiya and Nittaya J Kotchabhakdi 2004, Child and Youth Participation in Community: children development program in Mahasawat Subdistrict. Report paper. Department of Pediatrics, Faculty of Medicine, Ramathibodi Hospital, Mahidol University, Salaya, Nakornpathom, Thailand

Chapter 5
Australia

Jan Mason and Natalie Bolzan

Introduction

Australia is a federation comprising six states (New South Wales, Queensland, South Australia, Tasmania, Victoria and Western Australia) and two territories (Australian Capital Territory and Northern Territory). At the time of the 2006 census, Australia's population was approximately 20 million people and was growing at a rate of 1.5% per annum (ABS 2007). Children aged 0–14 years represent almost 20% of Australia's population (ABS 2007).

Australia's population has been described as 'largely homogenous, urban and predominately Christian' (Wikipedia 2007). However, the country's colonial history and comparatively high levels of migration have resulted in a diversity of cultural backgrounds. While early settlement and post-war migration was dominated by people of Anglo-Celtic and European descent, recent migration has increasingly come from non-European countries. Indigenous Australians represent 2.3% of the total population (ABS 2007).

The Federal Government holds the main revenue collecting powers, while the Department of Families, Community Services and Indigenous Affairs has some responsibility for children's issues. However, most of the administration of children's issues occurs at the state level through a number of education, community and child welfare agencies.

Australia has been described as 'a rich country with a relatively well-educated population, good public services, well-developed democratic institutions, low levels of corruption and a tradition of acceptance and egalitarianism' (Sidoti 2004, p. 34). However, as Sidoti (2004) argues, over the last decade, the Australian Government's promotion of human rights, including those of children, has come under scrutiny both nationally and internationally due to a general retreat on issues of social justice and human rights.

Ratification and implementation of CRC

Australia ratified the United Nations Convention on the Rights of the Child (CRC) in late 1990. However, as the Australian Government has not yet enacted any legislation to implement the CRC, its effects remain indirect (NGO Report 2005). The government is required to submit a report to the UN on the implementation of the CRC, while an alternative report is also submitted by a coalition of non-government organisations. The 2005 non-government report on Australia's implementation of the convention argued that the Australian Government 'now seems inclined to retreat from its commitment to the Convention' (NGO Report 2005, p. xii) and that, in relation to the principle of child participation, 'there are significant restrictions and tokenistic or manipulative processes in some important areas' (NGO Report 2005, p. xiii). Despite limited implementation at the federal level, some states have included principles relevant to the convention in their legislation. In New South Wales the *Children and Young Persons (Care and Protection) Act 1998* (NSW) and section ten of the *Adoption Act 2000* (NSW) give statutory force to Article 12, while child protection legislation in the Australian Capital Territory, in South Australia and Queensland also reflect Article 12 (Lawstuff 2008).

The study

In the Australian component of the international research described in this book, complementary qualitative techniques—a literature and policy review and interviews with policymakers and children—were used to explore the ways in which the participatory principles are implemented in Australia, specifically in New South Wales. The researchers examined the ways in which the participation of children and young people in Australia is presented in readily accessible policy documents and associated literature. As a number of organisations in Australia promote the way children participate in their programs on the web as well as in other literature, a review of these sources provided important information on the state of children's participation in Australia.

The information obtained from these sources related to policies at the three main levels of government—national, state and local—and to some non-government initiatives. While a majority of the examples at state and local levels are from New South Wales, some pertinent examples from other Australian states have been included. Examples of participation are from the areas of education, health and community services. Reports from previous surveys or direct interviews with children about participation (e.g. in schools and out-of-home care) have been included where the data is relevant. Examples of children's participation in the major social institution of the family were not readily available in the literature.

Individual interviews were conducted with eight policymakers, while 23 children and young people (13 boys and 10 girls, all aged 14 to 16) were interviewed through six small focus groups. While some problems were initially experienced gaining access to the children, due to competing demands on schools, these focus groups were finally established at a small number of government schools. In the groups, the children worked together on drawings that responded to the focus questions. In this chapter what children contributed in these groups was supplemented in some instances by findings from reports on previous studies; these are then woven together with findings from the literature, and contributions of the policymakers. The research process of both secondary and primary data collection was completed in late 2005.

Findings

Four major and connected findings were drawn from the data arising from the literature and interviews. These findings are as follows:
1. The United Nations Convention on the Rights of the Child (UNCROC) principle of participation is implemented in Australia in inconsistent ways.
2. Generally, adults exercise control over which children can participate and the nature of their participation.
3. Children's participation is being defined in three different ways.
4. The way adult-child relations are structured in Australian society has significance for children's participation.

Inconsistencies in the implementation of the UNCROC principle of participation

The first major finding emerging from our analysis of child participation in Australia is that there are inconsistencies at all levels in the implementation of the UNCROC principle. For example, three states have Commissioners for Children and Young People, part of whose role is to encourage the participation of children and young people. However, other states and territories do not have a Commissioner and there is not, at the time of writing, one at the federal level. Inconsistencies are also evident in the way individual Australian states and territories have implemented requirements in state legislation for children to participate in major decisions about their lives. For example, in the early 21st century, New South Wales has been the only state whose adoption laws provided mechanisms for children's views to be taken into account in adoption decisions (Lawstuff 2008).

Inconsistencies are also evident in the ways in which national policies designed to implement the principle of children's participation are applied. For example, there are policy provisions in Australia for children to participate in the governance of schools directly, or through representatives, by being on committees such as School Councils, Curriculum Committees and Regional Boards, or through student-run Student Representative Councils and Junior School Councils. However, in practice, there is wide variation in the extent to which children's participation in such forums impacts on the practices within specific schools (Holdsworth 2005). Discussions with children and young people reflected inconsistencies within schools in the extent to which children experienced the application of principles of participation. In one school, many young people were dismissive of the role of the Student Representative Council (SRC). They spoke of it being totally controlled by the principal and as being a 'hollow' activity. Others at this school, however, drew attention to changes that had come about as a result of the SRC. For example, rules about school uniform had changed to reflect a diversity of student preferences. At the broader community level, while some young people mentioned they had participated in youth councils conducted by local government, other students were unaware that such opportunities existed.

Perhaps the greatest inconsistency was reported between the nature and extent of participation in public forums, such as school and community forums, and participation in the private forum of the family. Children informed us that they had more opportunity to participate in decision making within the family than in other forums. According to some children, participation in family decision making often occurred because parents realised that without such participation, children would act independently. Other children considered that there was a genuine respect within their individual families for them as autonomous actors.

Adult control over which children can participate and the issues they can participate in

A second major finding of the Australian research is that, in formal participatory forums, adults exert control over what issues children can participate in, at which ages they can participate, and sometimes even which individual children can participate. In these forums, the decisions in which adults involve young people as participants tend to be those categorised as 'youth issues'. Rarely do adults involve children in decision making on issues seen to impact on the wider community. For example, young people are consulted through youth councils in relation to community matters directly concerning youth, such as skate parks, but are not consulted on decisions about community spaces or issues affecting businesses in the area.

Some evidence suggests that adults limit child participation in schools to those young people who agree with adult perspectives and whom adults consider will represent their school or community favorably. As a consequence, many young people are being excluded from participating in these forums (Holdsworth 2005). Children told us that at school 'we have very little opportunity to choose for ourselves ... We get to choose sports and electives'. Children said that while they could have a say about what food should be sold in the canteen, they had less opportunity to contribute to educational issues, such as curriculum and teaching methods. For some children, this meant that 'teachers make us stick to the school curriculum and bore us silly'.

Likewise, discussions with the children revealed that opportunities to engage in decision making within the family were mostly limited to more mundane issues affecting them directly, rather than issues of a more general nature. The children told us that 'at home we pick clothing, sometimes food', and 'choose when friends come over', but stated that they had limited opportunity to participate in longer term decisions, such as where the family lived.

Age appears to be the characteristic most commonly employed by adults to determine which children will be allowed to participate. In effect, the evidence suggests that those children who most commonly participate in forums with adults are those who are nearest to adulthood in terms of age. This finding emerged most clearly from descriptions of the ages of children participating on various boards and programs. Indeed, the term 'young people' was used ambiguously in the literature, at times extending into the period legally regarded as adult (e.g. up to the age of 25). The ages of those participating in the National Youth Roundtable range from 15 to 24. Of the 50 young people participating in the Roundtable in 2004, the average age was 20 years, with only 13 persons being under the age of 18 (NGO Report 2005). In 2001–2, there were only three young people under 18 in the National Indigenous Leadership Group and none in the 2002–3 and 2003–4 groups (NGO Report 2005). In contrast, the NSW Commission for Children and Young People includes somewhat younger people in its reference group, with one young person being 13 years old and the rest aged between 14 and 17 (NSW Commission for Children and Young People 2006).

Children under 12 are still generally excluded from participating in most national and state-level forums. Most of the policymakers interviewed for this study considered that children's lack of mature cognitive skills made it difficult to involve them as participants. A very small number of policymakers discussed the importance of extending participation to young children. These policymakers believed that adults have a responsibility to develop the skills required to enable younger, even pre-verbal, children to be included as participants. The young people we talked with also identified

that adults equate age with the wisdom and experience necessary to participate constructively in decision making.

The focus on older young people to represent children generally ensures
that those included as participants in mainstream forums are those most
like adults in their interactions, meaning that adults do not have to engage
with difference. An outcome of these practices is that younger adults are
now, for some forms of participation, being defined as young people and
are potentially thereby being categorised as having non-adult status.

We could not determine from our analysis of either primary or secondary data any significant differences in participation according to gender
and/or race. The focus on cognitive ability and the ability to articulate, as
factors determining who participates, can certainly be interpreted as likely
to exclude socio-economically marginalised young people, including Indigenous young people. On the other hand, some marginalised young people
are specifically targeted by participatory forums, such as the Super Participation Learning Action Team (Daly et al. 2004) and CREATE Foundation. In Australia there are different opportunities for young people's participation, some more effective than others and most of them excluding
those young people under the ages of 12 or 14.

Definitions of child participation

The third finding concerns the actual definition of, or what is meant by,
child participation. In the literature, and from interviews with policymakers, we found that two separate definitions of child participation were
evident. These were an understanding of child and youth participation as
'taking part in' activities and an understanding of child and youth participation as having an influence on decision making. Children and young people
also understood participation as being about influencing; however, they
also described what appeared to be a third definition. This definition was
about children and young people considering they had an obligation to
contribute to activities for the benefit of others, such as family and the
community.

• Participation as 'taking part in'

The definition of participation which we describe as 'taking part in' is
about children being involved as participants in adult-determined activities, without having power to influence decisions or processes. Implicit in
this definition is an understanding that, by participating, children are being
educated, frequently in terms of becoming future citizens. Some policymakers believed that children and young people were satisfied if they were
involved in processes in which they had a chance to express their views.

Based on descriptions provided online, examples of programs that appear to align with the approach of 'taking part in' include the Australian
CROC Eisteddfod, (which is about encouraging students to be involved in

music and drama), the Green Corps (which involves young people aged 17 to 20 in addressing environmental issues) and the Australian Defence Cadets (which encourages young people to learn physical skills and increase their fitness). In these programs, young people take part in activities designed for them by adults, without themselves having direct influence on the structure or composition of the program. An aim that is implicit in some of these programs (i.e. of providing children and young people with opportunities to learn skills relevant to citizenship) is made explicit in programs conducted by the Parliamentary Education Office. This office has created ways of young people taking part in various activities designed to educate them to be part of democratic forums when they become adults. These include Kidsview, an interactive website that helps to enhance children's knowledge of the parliamentary process, and organised visits to Parliament House, with opportunities to debate a bill in a mock House of Representatives.

- **Participation as children and young people influencing decision making**

A second definition of participation articulated by some policymakers and children concerns children influencing decision making. As described by both policymakers and children, this definition was about adults and children collaborating in decision making and children's contributions affecting decisions. For example, the children we talked with for this research project defined child participation as meaning engagement that makes an impact, as in, 'When someone has a say to an outcome of a situation'. The crucial element in defining participation for the children we interviewed was having 'choice'. At the level of community decision making, children considered their participation was crucial in influencing outcomes about what to do or provide for young people. These comments reflected a similar way of thinking about child participation in decision making to that described by children and young people in an earlier New South Wales study. In this study, children and young people emphasised the importance of children's decision making about their out-of-home care being taken seriously (NSW Child Protection Council 1998).

In the Australian literature, and in discussions with policymakers, the notion of participation as being about influencing decisions is usually most marked in participatory activities for more marginalised young people. An example of this approach is the Queensland Super Participation Learning Action Team (SPLAT). In this initiative of the Queensland Department of Communities, the service provider collaborated with service recipients to assist eight young people to develop the skills required to participate in a review of the delivery of care to young people. They established a foundation for ongoing engagement of young people in care as 'colleagues' or collaborators with the service delivery system (Daly, McPherson & Reck 2004).

Another example of a program that defines child participation as influencing events and decision making is the CREATE Foundation. CREATE is 'an organisation run for and by children and young people in out-of-home care and those that have previously been in out-of-home care' (CREATE 2004, p. 1). This organisation has developed a Bill of Rights for children and young people in care, and has assisted them to share their stories and to participate in forums to inform policymakers and practitioners about issues impacting on children and young people in out-of-home care. Having choice and negotiating decisions to meet children's individual needs was also emphasised as being of importance to children in research on children's needs in care (Mason & Gibson 2004). Some states have Children's Commissions with a focus on involving children and young people as participants influencing decision making. Some of the documents of the New South Wales Commission for Children and Young people published on the internet provide information to the community on involving children and young people in ways that can influence practice. These include *Taking PARTicipation seriously* (2001), *Participation: sharing the stage* (2002) and *Taking participation seriously—researching with children and young people* (2005).

The Australia Council for the Arts is an example of one of the few organisations with a broad community focus that appears to have an inclusive approach to children and young people as participants in decision making. The Council states that they see their role as 'supporting, promoting and raising the profile of artistic and creative work by, for and with young people and children'. They envisage that 'this policy—and the work of young people supported in response to it—will influence future planning of all programs of the Australia Council' (2004, p. 4f).

• Participation as an obligation

A third definition of participation was articulated by children and young people in our discussions with them. This definition was not evident in the literature or in the interviews with policymakers. This definition is about children feeling an obligation to contribute as participants, whether in the family or the broader community. This definition differed from the adult definition of 'taking part in' in that it was about responsibility in the present, rather than becoming responsible or good citizens in the future. Young people in this research spoke of helping out, working together, 'contributing', 'doing your share', having a responsibility to 'pitch in and do your bit'. These children and young people appeared to value what they had to offer in the present and believed they could make contributions as members of civic society.

Structural barriers to participation by children and young people

Children and young people identified structural barriers to their participation in existing relations between adults and children, as well as in laws that prevent children from voting, driving and drinking.

Young people in our group discussions described how differences in power between adults and children can prevent children from participating and may deny them decision making opportunities. They described the attitude of adults as fundamental to the lack of opportunities for children to participate, as such attitudes often meant that younger people are not trusted or valued and have a lesser social standing. This was particularly evident in decision making in the public domain. Young people commented that 'old people make choices for young people' and gave as an example a skate park, which 'was good until they (adults) took over'. Some young people described the structural nature of power inequalities between adults and young people as occurring because children have a 'lack of communication with people in power'. Others described how 'no-one listens to teenagers'.

At the family level, parent-child relations were described as more complex. One young person considered that 'in personal decisions, older people such as relatives believe they know what's best and may stop you doing your own thing'. Some young people considered that while parents often had more power than children and young people, it was possible for children to resist and challenge this power. One young person stated that 'parents stop us because they have the power, although they eventually give up'.

Some young people described how laws, such as those about voting age, resulted in them feeling excluded as they limited their access to public decision making forums. Further, some children stated that they experienced restrictions to their participation due to a lack of services, such as transport. Young people described how frustration over this exclusion sometime resulted in them committing acts of vandalism, breaking the law, lying, getting into trouble or simply 'sneaking out'. They considered that such exclusion wasted significant resources, stating that 'skills and abilities go unused and unacknowledged and may be used in a bad way'.

The children and young people discussed attitudes that facilitated their participation, such as being 'thought of by adults as near equals', being 'allowed to a have a say', and 'being made to feel welcome'. They considered that such experiences had a transformative role in terms of children's status, as they meant 'be(ing) accepted [at a] higher place'. Such comments suggested that young people saw participation as being about inclusion in the community and an improvement in their status through an acceptance into the adult domain.

Conclusion

The key findings about participation policies and practices, as evident from our research, indicate that while the concept of participation is broadly embraced, there is frequently a difference between how children and young people define participation and how some adults define it. While the dominant definition of participation used by children (i.e. as contributing in ways that influence decisions) is a definition used by some adults, the majority of adults defined participation differently. Adult definitions, as indicated in interviews or in adult contributions to websites and documents, constructed children's participation in terms of children being 'part of' activities. Many considered that much of the value of these activities was in training for children's futures. Some other adults defined participation in ways similar to the way in which children and young people generally defined it; that is, as influencing decisions. Additionally, some young people posited an understanding of what participation is about that extended the definitions used by adults. These young people understood themselves as members of families and society, and as having opinions and indeed obligations to contribute from their experiences and knowledge. This difference in the way children and adults defined participation is fundamental in explaining some of the limitations children and young people confront in being able to constructively influence either decisions in their own lives, or in the society in which they are living.

In Australia young people who are advantaged in some respects (e.g. age and abilities) may be able to have some input into some aspects of broad policymaking. Additionally, young people who are marginalised may be able, in some special instances, to have input into decisions about their own lives and the lives of those who are similarly marginalised. Conversely, children or younger young people are virtually excluded from public decision making and from providing input on matters outside of what adults have defined as 'youth issues'.

Children recognised that the way in which adult-child relations are structured in Australia frequently acts as a barrier to their participation, and that this may result in resistance and protest behavior. They also gave examples of ways in which adults can build bridges that provide children with opportunities to participate constructively. Such bridging can have a transformative effect on the social position of children in their families and in broader society.

Acknowledgements

We wish to thank Samia Michail who did much of the research for this chapter as well as the policy makers and children who contributed through interviews and focus groups.

References

Australian Bureau of Statistics 2007, Catalogue 2068.0, 2006 census of population and housing viewed 23 October 2007, <http://www.abs.gov.au>.

Australia Council 2003, *Young people and the arts policy*, Commonwealth of Australia.

CREATE Foundation 2004, *Being our best! A report on Australia's young people in care*, August 2004, Strawberry Hills, NSW.

Daly, W, McPherson, C & Reck, L 2004, 'SPLAT: a model of young people's participation that moves beyond the rhetoric to empowerment', *Children Australia*, vol. 29 (4), pp. 20–26.

Holdsworth, R 2005, 'Taking young people seriously means giving them serious things to do', in J Mason and T Fattore (eds), *Children taken seriously. In theory, policy and practice*, Jessica Kingsley, London, 2005.

Lawstuff, 'What's up CROC ? Australia's implementation of the Convention on the Rights of the Child (CROC), viewed 5 September 2008, <http://www.ncylc.org.au/croc/crocbenefits.html>.

Mason, J and Gibson, C 2004, *The needs of children in care: a report,* Non-Government Report. The implementation of the United Nations Convention on the Rights of the Child in Australia, May 2005.

NSW Child Protection Council 1998, *Having a say*, NSW Child Protection Council, Sydney.

NSW Commission for Children and Young People 2006, Viewed 3 November 2006, <http://www.kids.nsw.gov.au/about/ref-group.html>.

Sidoti, C 2004, 'Human rights: Australia's lost plot', in R. Leonard (ed.), *A fair go: some issues of social justice in Australia,* Common Ground Press, Altona.

Chapter 6
Sri Lanka

Swarna Wijetunge

Introduction

Sri Lanka is a tropical island located in the Indian Ocean. Throughout re-corded history, Sri Lanka (known as Ceylon until 1972) has been under monarchical rule. The country became a colonial entity when the coastal areas first came under the rule of the Portuguese (1505–1658), followed by the Dutch (1658–1796) and the British (1796–1815). With the fall of the interior kingdom of Kandy in 1815, the entire country came under British rule.

After 443 years of colonial rule, Ceylon gained independence in 1948. In 1972, it became a republic and is now known as the Democratic Socialist Republic of Sri Lanka. The country now has a parliamentary system of government and since 1978 has been governed under a Republican Constitution. The executive power of the Sri Lanka Government is vested in the President, while the parliament is responsible for legislation. Administratively, the country is divided into nine provinces and 25 districts. Subsequent to the 1978 Constitution, the 13th Amendment to the Constitution was passed and certain powers were devolved to the nine provinces by the establishment of Provincial Councils.

The provisional total population of Sri Lanka in 2005 was approximately 19 million (Central Bank of Sri Lanka 2006). In 2006, the annual growth rate of the population was 1.0%. The male-female ratio of the population is approximately 49:51 (Central Bank of Sri Lanka 2006). According to the census of 2001 (which could not be conducted in the Northern province and part of the Eastern province, due to the prevailing conflict situation), the distribution of the population by ethnicity is as follows: Sinhalese 81.9%, the Sri Lankan Tamils 4.3%, Indian Tamils 5.1% and Muslims 8.0%. The distribution by religion is: Buddhists 76.6%, Islamic 8.5%, Hindus 7.9%, Roman Catholics 6.1% and Christians 0.8%. Life expectancy at birth is 74.0 years and the Life Expectancy Index is 0.82. Real GDP per Capita is 3,778 (PPP $) and the GDP Index is 0.61. The Human Development Index is 0.751 and the HDI rank is 93. In 1995, the proportion of the population living on less than US$1 a day was 66%, while the proportion living on less than US$2 a day was 45.5%. Mean household income per month (2003/2004) was Rs.17, 114. According to the Department of Census and Statistics, 22.7% of individuals and 19.2% of households stood below the poverty line in 2002. In 2005, the overall unemployment rate was 7.7%, with 5.5% of males unemployed and 11.9% of females unemployed. The literacy rate for females is 94.5, while for males it is 92.5. The Education Index is 0.83. The Education Attainment (2003–2004) was: No schooling: 7.9%, Primary: 29.9%, Secondary: 41.0% and Tertiary: 21.2%. In Sri Lanka, it is compulsory for children aged between 5 and 14 to attend school.

Ratification and implementation of the child rights charter

Sri Lanka ratified the child rights charter and the global plan of action in 1991. Based on the convention, a children's charter was also developed in Sri Lanka in 1991, which subsequently provided a framework for the modification of existing Sri Lanka law. A plan of action for children in Sri Lanka was also formulated, at the directive of the President. However, this has not been adequately and effectively implemented since 1993, as indicated by an analysis of the current situation relating to child rights (Save the Children, Sri Lanka 2003). The official position on the progress made in the sphere of child rights and their enforcement indicates noteworthy progress since 1995 (Second Country Report on the implementation of the convention of the rights of the child). The quantum of legislation and their areas of coverage are impressive, ranging from the Human Rights Commission Act, the National Child Protection Authority Act (NCPA) and Act No. 50 of 1998, through to the amendment of legislation in the penal code (Acts No. 22 of 1995 and No. 29 of 1998), and the instituting of special desks for children and women at police stations.

However, the machinery that has been set up for implementation and monitoring suffers from a lack of both human and financial resources, overlapping responsibilities and inadequate public awareness of the changes. For example, when undertaking the child rights situation analysis (CRSA), the Sri Lanka research group Save the Children found that many parents and teachers were unaware of the roles of the NCPA and DCPC (District

Child Rights Protection Committees). The two major agencies for child protection, namely the National Child Protection Authority and the Department of Probation and Child Care Services, run parallel monitoring systems, leading to many overlaps (Commissioner, Department of Probation and Child Care Services 2003, interviewed by Save the Children researchers). Furthermore, the attendance of the nominated members of the national monitoring committees is irregular; this impacts upon the effectiveness of the process essential for bringing outside opinion and views to bear upon the implementation of laws and policies.

Child participation

Child participation, in the sense and terminology of the UN child rights charter definition, is currently being advocated in Sri Lanka and practiced with varying degrees of success by the INGO and NGO sectors. Some of the most notable organisations in this field include UNICEF, Save the Children Sri Lanka and Plan Sri Lanka. UNICEF currently advocates Child Friendly Schools, which campaigns for the right of children to a genuinely child-centered school. The most recent initiative of Save the Children Sri Lanka has been the Children's Consultation in Education project, which targeted tsunami affected areas. The consultation process included children as researchers and one of the project's aims was child-empowerment. Plan Sri Lanka engages the participation of children in all their programs, from project conceptualisation and right throughout the project cycle. Many others working in the NGO sector have enabled child participation in the sense of 'participation in decision making in matters that affect their lives'.

One notable government initiative was the consultative process initiated by the government and facilitated by Sarvodaya and UNICEF to get children's participation in the formulation of the National Plan of Action for the Children of Sri Lanka 2004–2008. Eight workshops were held at the provincial level for children between the ages of 14 and 18 years. The children were selected from children's organisations and children's clubs. Children from differently abled groups and street children were also included in the group of representatives, so that the National Plan of Action might reflect the concerns, issues and problems of children with a wide spectrum of backgrounds and highlight the solutions as the children perceived them. The children in these organisations selected their representatives to the consultation, using gender, ethnicity and age as the criteria for selection. The issues and problems identified as affecting the children and the solutions proposed by the children were consolidated for further analysis and refinement at the pre-national forum, for submission to the government at the national forum. The children emphasised that they wanted to be the agents of their own development and wanted to participate fully, particularly in areas where they were directly affected. They wanted adults to listen more systematically to what they had to say and to provide the support necessary for them to gain greater control over their lives.

A similar initiative was the children's parliament held by the Save the Children Alliance of Sri Lanka in 2001, where nearly 11,000 children from all over the country, representing all groups and strata of society, came together to deliberate on matters concerning them. The government gave recognition to the issues raised in the children's parliament and agreed to incorporate the issues in the government's policy strategies.

The children of Sri Lanka

To attempt to introduce the 'children of Sri Lanka' would be impossible, for children, like women, do not form a homogenous social category: 'Childhood and the personal history of each child is defined by the material, historical, socio-cultural circumstances of their life, including the social systems, cultural beliefs and practices, political and legal environment ... gender, age, ethnicity, class, caste, religion are some of the factors which produce different conditions, and hence realities and experiences for different types of childhood' (Faruqi 1997, p. 3).

Nonetheless, how children's lives have changed with modern times and the influences that have shaped their lives bear recording, as perceptions of children have changed significantly from the past to the present. Whether rural or urban, children today are strongly influenced by the Western model (mostly American) of how children think and behave, irrespective of how hard parents and elders try to pull them away from Western influences and attempt to maintain their cultural identity. In the global village, television and other media set the pace, and children are open to varied influences in keeping up with other children and young people of their generation. This is certainly the case with many children in Sri Lanka, although the extent to which individual children are influenced by Western values depends on their upbringing. It is important that adults recognise that some compromise in this area is necessary to enable children to interact successfully with the changing social environment. Children learn to adapt, to retain cultural values that are fundamentally and morally timeless, and to disregard others that do not stand the test of rational scrutiny.

In Sri Lanka, as in many other Asian cultures, education is considered the key to success for any child, and therefore children are under tremendous pressure to achieve, to get the highest possible grades at public examinations, and to excel in other spheres as well. Because of this, parents often take great steps to ensure that that nothing interferes with their child's academic pursuits. This strongly mars children's efforts at participation; even everyday pursuits like meeting friends, going places and having fun are severely curtailed.

In parts of Sri Lanka, such as the Northern and Eastern provinces, most children and young people have known little else but war, destruction and trauma of every conceivable kind. They have shown remarkable resilience in the face of constant displacement, destruction and loss of human life. Child participation takes new and different forms in such situations, and many innovative initiatives are on record of children's and young people's resilience and participation. In these situations, children often mature early and are sometimes compelled to take matters into their own hands. As such, their opinions of child participation are likely to differ markedly from the views of children in other parts of the country. Unfortunately, children from the north and east could not be included in the present study, but their views are well documented in the literature.

The type of child most likely to provide the UN child rights charter version of what child participation means is the 'sophisticated' child: the urban, well-to-do child, who is articulate and well-informed. The present study deliberately omitted the category of the sophisticated child, for example, children who had participated internationally in children's parliaments or who had been articulate spokespersons for children in various forums. Such children were deemed exceptional and not representative of the typical Sri Lankan child.

The Study

The sample of children

The sample of children and young people (n=63) used for this study was drawn from six of the nine provinces of Sri Lanka, covering 10 of the 25 districts. Children were categorised into two age groups: 12–14 and 15–17. In the 12–14 age group, there were 20 males and 10 females. In the 15–17 age group, there were 17 males and 16 females. By ethnicity, there were 44 Sinhalese, seven Tamils, eight Muslims and two others of mixed parentage. The religions were also well-represented: 40 of the children were Buddhist, 10 were Islamic, six were Hindu, three were Catholic and four were Christian. This was a convenient sample, with teachers who were conducting research for the National Education Research and Evaluation Centre (NEREC), Faculty of Education, University of Colombo, volunteering to conduct focus group discussions in the various locations where research was being conducted. This ensured that children from both rural and urban locations and a good cross-section of children with varying backgrounds were engaged in these discussions. Opinions from parents, community leaders and experts were also solicited. Ministry of Education officials and a cross-section of the education community (including experts) who participated in a NEREC seminar were asked to respond in writing to the query 'What does children's and young people's participation mean to you?' However, in the following analysis, prominence is given to children's meanings and their understanding of participation in the light of UN assumptions.

Findings

What child participation means to children

There was considerable variation in the nature and range of meanings given by children and young people for 'children's and young people's participation'. For 27% of the children, participation meant '*participation in decision making*', although none categorically stated it as '*participation in decision making in what affects their lives*'. Another 16% of the children said that participation meant '*problem solving* and *contributing one's ideas/suggestions*'. Of the children and young people in the sample, 65% were more prone to define participation as '*taking part in*', with qualifiers such as '*actively taking part in*', '*engaging fully in*', and '*empowering to do things in own way*'. The children and young people also provided contexts of such participation, including participating as a member of the family (18%), participating in school, learning processes or educational activities (14%), and participating in societal activities (19%) such as religious activities or various organised social groups.

There was a semantic limitation to conceptualising what participation meant. In the local languages (e.g. in Sinhala), the term for participation (*sahabagithvaya*) means '*to join in/ participate with others*'. The children wanted more clarification on the researcher's use of the term participation, but the researchers had been specifically instructed to give no further clarification, as the whole idea was to get children's meanings. Culturally, the term *sahabagithvaya* is used in the literal sense of 'joining in with others' or 'take part in', with stress on the group and not so much the individual. Therefore, for 65% of the children, participation was contextual; thus family, school, social and cultural activities they *take part in* came to the forefront when they thought of participation.

The opportunities children get to participate

The contexts that the children and young people indicated, in defining their participation, were enlarged on by them in response to the question 'What opportunities do you and children/young people in families like yours get to participate?' The most frequently mentioned opportunities were participation as a member of the family (48%) including the family's economic activities, and participation in school contexts, such as in educational (25%) and co-curricular (62%) activities such as sports. Within the 'cultural' cluster of opportunities (identified by 67% of children), festivals and religious activities took prominence. Social work (21%), clubs and societies (22%), and leisure time activities such as trips and hobbies (13%) were some of the other opportunities for participation that the children referred to. It is interesting to note that economic activities, apart from those included in 'participation in family activities', were referred to by only one child; likewise, politics was also referred to by only one young person as an opportunity for participation. In the context of how children's lives are ordered, with priority often given to studies to the exclusion of all else, these responses are understandable; the children we consulted all attended school, and apart from economic activities conducted in a family context, children's concerns were mostly to do with school and 'cultural' activities.

Limits to children's and young people's participation in families

The question about what limited children's and young people's participation received many and varied responses from the children themselves. In an inclusive cluster of responses that the researcher labeled broadly as *'parental, family and adults' attitudes toward children and young people'*, there were a number of more specific sub-clusters, such as *'strong/rigid parental attitudes'* (44%) and *'precautionary custodial measures'* (22%) that children identified as preventing them from participating. Fear on the part of parents and other adults in the family that children and young people will get distracted from their studies, get into trouble, go astray, or disgrace the family were most frequently stated as limiting children's opportunities to participate. Some children claimed that parents and adults do not have faith or trust in their abilities (17%), do not give them leadership opportunities, and discourage them from participating; one respondent stated categorically that parents and adults have "no regard for children's rights". Some respondents considered the *'personality characteristics and immaturities'* of children and young persons themselves as factors that limit participation, such as a lack of self-confidence, inexperience, or the inability to engage successfully in an activity.

Another cluster of limitations was categorised as *'practical constraints'*; factors associated with the competitive education system, extra-school tuition, examination pressures and health reasons belonged in this list. Viewing TV, school workload and security-related concerns were other practical constraints identified. Finally, in a cluster categorised as *'external impediments'*, there were references to societal acceptance, political influence, school rules and regulations, and the influence of friends.

Factors encouraging children's and young people's participation

Factors connected with adults predominated in the responses to this question. *More positive and democratic parent child relationships/encouragement in school etc. by adults* was the response category with the highest agreement. Furthermore, the children's appeal for *some degree of acceptance of children's/young people's ideas and suggestions without outright rejection* complemented their need for understanding and encouragement by adults. Children asked that *children's participation be permitted, that they be made aware of the import-ance of participation,* and *that their engagement be facilitated and appreciated.* For example, the children requested that they be given opportunities to assume leadership roles and asked that adults have faith in their abilities. The chil-dren in the survey also suggested that getting to know the experiences of adults, peer groups and other children would enhance their participation. They believed that increased parental participation would set them an ex-ample, and if their inadequacies were pointed out, they would benefit by such guidance.

Children and young people also turned an inward eye, situating the locus of control within the self. Self-confidence, readiness to face chal-lenges, a need to get to know society, curiosity, interest, and competitive-ness—in short, *their own attitudes and inclinations*—were specified by chil-dren and young people as factors influencing their participation. Some chil-dren also looked to *external rewards*, such as opportunities to obtain quali-fications and monetary and other incentives, to demonstrate their capabilities.

Finally, some children and young people focused on *aspects of personal de-velopment* that would contribute to their enhanced participation, including fine-tuning their talents and capabilities and developing skills in managing interpersonal relationships (e.g. making friends and cooperating with other people).

Problems in participation

The responses related to any perceived problems with children's participa-tion can be categorised into four groups: a categorical 'yes' or 'no', a condi-tional 'sometimes' and 'rarely'. Those who categorically said there are prob-lems with participation cited breakdowns in parent-child relationships, in-appropriate relationships or associations, and addictions. One respondent noted that adults find it difficult to answer some of the questions children ask today. In contrast, in the categorical 'no' response cluster, respondents said that children's and young people's participation is beneficial to adults and that participation enables creative problem solving. Many issues were raised in the conditional response categories, such as misunderstandings, suspicion, and conflicts arising from a clash of ideas, opinions and atti-tudes. The perennial accusations that parents and adults often discourage children's participation, divert children to other activities, do not facilitate participation opportunities, or blame children when a task is not accom-plished satisfactorily were all cited as triggers causing problems with chil-dren's participation. Children and young people also acknowledged that their own inexperience, their lack of skill in working systematically, and their lack of work ethics such as time management can create problems with their participation.

Benefits of children's and young people's participation

In response to the question about the benefits of children's participation, the children and young people identified many positive developmental (personal and relational) benefits; these responses have been clustered inclusively in the category *'personal development'*. It is interesting to note that the release of inhibitions regarding speaking up and exchanging one's ideas, developing one's ability to make the right decisions, and gaining experience were among the leading benefits cited in this cluster.

Gaining the confidence to face problems and challenges, developing talents, gaining popularity, creating self-satisfaction, and developing skills in management were some of the other benefits cited. Learning about life and the world, and thereby developing one's ability to act according to contemporary needs whilst serving one's own needs, was another sub-cluster within this broad category of *personal development*. The children also stated that new learning and creative skills and generating new ideas toward solving problems were general benefits they would derive from participation. In the process, they expected to acquire qualifications for the future, which may have the potential to lead to economic benefits.

Conclusion

Some of the variables used in this study require closer analysis: these include gender, age, ethnicity and rural/urban residency.

The gender representation of males to females in the sample was 37:26. In the discussions, however, the girls were very vocal, compensating for being outnumbered by the boys. It is interesting that the issue of gender was not commonly registered in the opinions of the children; it was more their rights and perceptions as children that came across. One lone mother commented on the necessity of protecting female children after they reach puberty. A 12-year old girl commented on her parents 'not allowing her to go unaccompanied'. Parents gave their version of children's and young people's participation, particularly referring to the limits they had imposed, such as curtailing 'unnecessarily hanging out with friends' and 'not allowing decisions to be made without exercising caution', with no mention of the gender of the child. In Sri Lanka, gender parity is seen in many spheres of activity such as education and ensuring the rights of the child.

In fact, parental expectation of female children is very high, especially in relation to education.

The two age categories selected, 12–14 and 15–17, showed some differences in their responses, but this varied according to the maturity and experiences of the children. A 14-year-old Tamil boy attending a prestigious boy's school in Colombo reported that 'my parents have limited my participation to sports and education'. On the other hand, there was a 15-year-old who insisted that participation means the 'obligation to do what we can for the family and school'; he cited, as an example, 'the right to participate in parental and siblings' problems' as a member of the family, whereas, in practice, this is often curtailed. Specific mention was made by the children of the younger age group of not only parents but also their 'older brothers and sisters trying to dominate them'. It was revealed that older brothers and sisters constantly reminded and ridiculed them, and cited instances where a decision made by the younger sibling went wrong. This constant domination often resulted in damage to children's personalities.

Ethnicity in the Sri Lankan context is a significant variable and it was ensured that all ethnic groups were represented in this sample. However, ethnicity, like gender, only registered marginally in the voices of the children. A Tamil boy mentioned that language is a barrier to the participation of ethnic groups in Sri Lanka. The fact that most young people in Sri Lanka today have grown up studying in the medium of their mother tongue means that relatively few have proficiency in any other language/s, including English. In this study, the survey questions were translated into Sinhalese and Tamil (the two national languages) and the respondents were asked at the beginning of the discussion which language they were most comfortable with. The English version of the questions was also made available. The responses, therefore, collectively, were in all three languages: Sinhalese, Tamil and English.

The rural-urban factor was left open in the sampling process; in Sri Lanka, the people located in municipalities and urban council areas are considered urban, and all others (i.e. provincial council areas) are considered rural. The researchers ensured that children located in both areas were represented in the sample. In a few instances, children mentioned the lack of finances as a barrier to participation, and in this group there were both urban and rural children. The agricultural cycle in the villages often disrupts the education of rural children, but they defined it as participation in parental livelihoods and an obligation that they were required to meet. Poverty, on the other hand, was identified as a significant factor preventing the full participation of children.

Finally, the adult respondents gave a variety of responses to their definition of children's and young people's participation. Those in the 'expert' category (policy makers and senior officials), who were aware of the rights approach, all gave similar responses, and were cautious of children's and young people's right to participate in decision making in matters that affect their lives. For example, the increasing display of student violence in schools was often cited by members of this group as demonstrating a need for caution in adopting a rights-based approach. The resistance to the introduction of school parliaments and other such liberal moves in school management clearly shows that this concept of child participation is viewed by some experts in the education system as being 'ahead of its time'.

In Asian cultures, the adult-child relationship has always been one of deference to elders and, by and large, this relationship structure remains. In cultures where the community and family, not the individual, come first, resistance to the rights-based approach to participation is to be expected. The children's perception of participation as an obligation more than a right is in keeping with this cultural perspective. As one 15-year-old stated, participation is 'the obligation to do what we can for the family and school'. A strictly rights-based approach seems more of a Western-oriented concept as, throughout Sri Lanka's history, children have been contributing members of Sri Lankan society in a more meaningful and inclusive sense than is commonly understood by the modern (particularly the Western) conception of participation.

References

Central Bank of Sri Lanka 2006, Economic and social statistics of Sri Lanka. http://www.cbsl.gov.lk/info/10_publication/p_2.htm (accessed 16th October 2009)

Department of Census and Statistics, Sri Lanka 2005, Statistical pocket book of Sri Lanka. http://data.un.org/CountryProfile.aspx?crName=Sri%20Lanka (accessed 16th October 2009)

Faruqi, F 1997, Putting children first! Child rights, participation and development, in South and Central Asia's children, no. 8, Save the Children UK. www.crin.org/docs/resources/publications/.../ SCUK_**participation** (accessed 16th October 2009)

Save the Children, Sri Lanka 2003, Situation analysis of child rights.

UNDP 2004, Human development report.

UNICEF 2003, Child participation in Sri Lanka: a review of national policy, legislation and practice and comprehensive mapping of child participation initiatives in Sri Lanka.

(Sources: Human Development Report 2004, UNDP cited in Economic and Social Statistics of Sri Lanka, 2005, Central Bank of Sri Lanka; Annual Report 2005, Central Bank of Sri Lanka; Poverty statistics / Indicators for Sri Lanka, Department of Census and Statistics; Statistical pocket book – 2005, Sri Lanka, Department of Census and Statistics).

Chapter 7
Summary of Findings

Anil Kumar

Introduction

The convention on the rights of the child which was adopted by the United Nations in 1989 has been ratified almost universally and the governments of the countries which participated in the research reported in this book have established laws and/or regulations to protect child rights as specified in the Convention. However, the overall findings of our research on child participation indicated that in the Asia-Pacific region countries in which our study was situated the principle of child participation as a right for children to have their views heard was not operationalised to any significant extent.

The meanings of 'child participation' and its cultural context

Analysis of our data pointed to two major and inter-related findings. These were, firstly, that there is considerable variation in meanings ascribed to the concept of child participation across countries in the Asia-Pacific region and, secondly, that the dominant construction of the concept of child participation was about children 'taking part in' activities.

It was clear that variations in the meanings of child participation were influenced by the different cultural and ideological contexts in which the research was conducted. Differences in the meanings of the concept 'child participation' became clear as the research progressed, but were initially camouflaged by the use of the English language as a means of communication amongst those of us conducting the research. As we continued our discussions around the data we developed more understanding of differences in the way we as researchers were using the concept of children 'taking part in'. For example, the way this term was being used by our Sri Lankan and Thai researchers and their research respondents meant an emphasis, in the use of the term, on children participating *with others,* as a group. In contrast the way our Australian researchers and their research respondents were using the term 'taking part in' was about children participating *as individuals* in adult organised activities. Arriving at an understanding of this confusion enabled us to more effectively comprehend the findings from the different countries.

Children's participation as 'taking part in'

This was the most common meaning attached to the term child participation. In all countries there was a general understanding of child participation as meaning children 'taking part in activities', although the specifics of what this meant varied across countries. In Asian countries such as Sri Lanka, participation as children 'taking part in' referred mainly to home and community building activities in association with adults, whereas, in Australia, reference to participation in community activities was related to more child-focused activities, such as recreational pursuits. While the community was the focus of child participation in Sri Lanka and Thailand, in India and China there was an emphasis on participation around family and school activities.

Children's participation as a right

There was a minor theme of understanding child participation as a right. However, this was a much more contested understanding. There was a limited focus on participation as a right in some of the countries where there was a strong NGO influence, such as Sri Lanka and India, which were subjected to long-standing Western influences. In China, where the government's one-child policy is changing the way childhood is being understood, issues regarding children's right to participate are beginning to be discussed. In Australia, some respondents perceived the idea of child participation as a right in rhetorical rather than practical terms, particularly at the level of policy. At a general level, analysis around the meaning of child participation as a right served to highlight the conflict between those countries or groups who espoused liberalist, individualist ideologies and those who were part of more collectivist traditions. These two ideological approaches generally contributed to different constructions of adult-child relations and, therefore, understandings of child participation. In Asian countries the traditionally strong and explicit focus on concepts of responsibility to family and community, in conjunction with the hierarchical organisation in these societies, can be seen to have contributed to an understanding of child participation as interacting with children's 'obligation' to community.

Children's participation as decision making

Associated with child participation as a right was a minor theme regarding children's right to be involved in decision making. In countries such as Sri Lanka and Thailand, participation around decision making was discussed as occurring within a context of responsibility to family and community. In Australia, India and also to a limited extent in China, child participation in decision making was applied mostly to family interactions around clothes, family consumption and extra-curricular activities.

In Australia, there was reasonably strong rhetoric around the participation of children in decision making at policy levels. However, there was often a gap between rhetoric and practice.

• Adult concerns promoting the principle of child participation

Some adults in all countries expressed concerns about promoting child participation. Adults in the Sri Lankan expert group adopted a cautious attitude to a rights based approach to participation, considering that it may contribute to an increase in student political violence, inappropriate relationships and associations, and the breakdown of parent child relationships. Within the range of opinions amongst those adults who contributed to the Indian study, some opposed implementation of the child participation principle and others endorsed it, along with the empowerment they associated with this principle. The study in Australia revealed that some adults believed that children should be consulted, particularly on youth issues. Generally, in the countries studied, there was an emphasis on participation as a means of socialising young people to be good future citizens.

• The influence of structural factors on child participation

Our analysis of the country findings indicated that the way existing adult-child relations are structured and the contexts in which these relations are situated in each country are highly significant for how 'child participation' is constructed.

Gender emerged from the analysis as an important factor in affecting which children could participate in what. Here, there was variation between countries. For example, while participation defined as 'taking part in' appeared to play only a marginal role in deciding the nature and extent of participation in Sri Lanka, in China participation of boys seemed greater than that of girls. In China, younger girls were described as 'taking part in' family activities while older girls took part in social activities. Similarly, in Thailand, opportunities for girls to participate were more focused on the home than was the case for boys, particularly as they became older. The Indian study indicated that girls were given fewer opportunities than boys, to participate. A major factor of this was the patriarchal nature of the society and the long standing societal attitude towards female participation. However, the situation in Australia showed no substantial difference between boys and girls in opportunities to participate. It was generally found that, as children become older and begin to be identified as young people (past 12 or 15), they have more opportunities to participate in families and the community.

Socio-economic factors and location were significant in determining participation in China and Thailand. In these countries, the data indicated that different types of participation were possible in urban and rural settings and these were influenced by socio-economic status. Generally, in Asian countries, rural or more working class children were likely to be required to, for example, participate in harvesting and farm work at times of increased demand, in line with the needs of the family and community. Findings from the Indian study indicated that its complex system of class, caste, religion, gender and location were important determinants of children's participation when defined as contributing to decision making.

Children's constructions of child participation

Children's constructions of child participation to a large extent paralleled adults' constructions, in the countries where the study was conducted, with some minor challenges to adult constructions occurring in all countries, these being more marked in India and Australia. In India, children highlighted, as an obstacle to their participation, an imbalance of power between adults and young people and the fact that children lacked the power to have their views heard. In Australia, young people's comments challenged policy makers' views that children and young people are satisfied if they are given the opportunity to be involved in processes in which they get a chance to express their views. Some young people indicated that simply taking part in such activities and processes is not enough. Further, some children in the Australian study presented a view of child participation, in line with collectivist thinking, of obligation to community. This contrasted with the individualist perspective of participation generally espoused in the study by adults in this country.

Summary

Overall, the findings tell us that children in the region are generally considered as participants in family and community life, with some differences in the way this is interpreted culturally, in terms of collectivist or individualist emphases. For the most part, understanding of child participation stopped short of being considered as a right of children and this impacted on their involvement in decision making. Further, the findings indicate that child participation is constrained by various structural factors, including adult-child power relations. The findings are significant in their potential to inform us about the tensions inherent in applying global principles cross-culturally.

Chapter 8
Applying a Concept Globally: What We've Learnt

Natalie Bolzan

Introduction

This research, begun in 2004, intended to investigate how children's participation, in line with the UN Convention on the Rights of the Child, was being implemented in five countries across the Asia-Pacific region. At various steps in this process we were confronted with challenges to this investigation which tested our thinking around what we were attempting to do. The researchers from the five countries worked through such fundamental differences as whether one research design needed to be replicated in five countries or whether it was necessary to allow five related or parallel projects to develop in response to local conditions. A recurring motif throughout the project was the need to clarify assumptions concerned with what we were doing and how we were doing it. Assumptions which needed to be explored ranged from the value placed on qualitative research data—through how adult-child relations were constructed to issues of who has power. We didn't set out to investigate whether children's participation was a concept suitable for global application, but this is the question we are left with.

It has been argued elsewhere that the UN Convention on the Rights of the Child emerged in part in response to a growing commitment to children's rights in line with a global trend towards democratisation creating a consensus that children's views should be taken seriously (Hinton 2008). The research reported here suggests that the UNCROC implementation may well be compromised by these broad assumptions.

The degree to which the convention has been adopted both formally and informally in the West is varied, but for citizens of those countries in the East for whom individual rights and democratic processes have less prominence, the meaning of children's participation has been revealed as being, at best, ambiguous and, at worst, imperialist. Not all countries have embraced democracy and Western liberal notions of individual rights in the same way. Factors such as history, political regimes, geographical imperatives and civil stability play a part in how social relations are configured and maintained. A framework premised on liberalism may require so much adjustment as to make it unrecognisable when transposed to a range of countries with cultures embedded in other traditions and ideologies. The joy of conducting this research was in the exploration and identification of where the spirit of UNCROC was evident across nations; the challenge was in identifying the form that spirit took.

Differences across the region

The research reported here has revealed that across the Asia-Pacific region there is no one meaning or understanding of children's participation. Indeed, there is often no one shared set of experiences or expectations of children's participation even within countries. Rather, there is a range of understandings which reflect the diversity of social relations across the region. Notions of childhood are not universal nor are constructions of family or community. Consequently, there is little consensus about what children's participation could mean.

The methodology, based on a partnership model, was pivotal in our being able to accommodate the different circumstances of each country as well as being able to understand the various countries' internal differences. Having the voice of researchers from within each country enabled a deep collaborative and comparative analysis of children's participation to take place. This has revealed points of divergence in understandings of children's participation that are rarely acknowledged. Even at the level of data collection, differences emerged around children's opportunity to participate. In Sri Lanka, particularly after the Tsunami which devastated the southern part of that country, children were easily and regularly accessed for their reaction to events and participation in research, in Australia, four separate gatekeepers needed to be negotiated in order to engage children in research.

The differential access to children even at the stage of data collection speaks to the differential opportunities for children to engage in activities even when they are of direct relevance. The data from Sri Lanka and Thailand placed emphasis on children contributing to the broad community (to do with political and environmental upheavals) whereas adults in the other countries believed child participation should be limited to contexts of family and school and, for India, to work situations as well. Adults in all countries bar Australia tended, to varying degrees, to consider that children had an obligation to participate—in terms of taking part in specific ways—rather than a right. In Australia, it was the young people who held the perspective of participation as an obligation. Australian adults tended to see children's participation as a right afforded them rather than the responsibility of children and young people. This hints at the differential positioning of children in countries across the region.

By working closely as a group and by constantly reflecting on what we were doing and saying, we were made aware of the more subtle influences which were impacting on children's participation—factors such as differences in the construction of childhood and in adult-child relations. In Sri Lanka and Thailand, children appeared to have a status connected to their membership of community. In India and China children are situated within circumscribed social locations of family, school and work, whilst, in Australia, children's participation is at the discretion of adults who frame participation broadly in terms of opportunities offered to children and young people and as practice for adulthood.

A further difference across the region centered on collectivist and individualist ideologies. In China, India, Thailand and Sri Lanka, responsibility to family and community has traditionally taken precedence over individual rights; an ethos of collectivism has been dominant. In these countries children have traditionally not received separate focus. India began to change in the early twentieth century with wider exposure to Western ideologies and the increasing nuclearisation of families contributing to a shift away from the group to the individual.

One feature common across the region was the dynamic nature of social structures and relations. Each country noted changes occurring. In China, the policies limiting the number of children per family to one was seen to have resulted in the greater valuing of children and as beginning to influence parent-child relations towards more recognition of children's rights. In India and Sri Lanka, where there has been significant involvement by NGOs in the implementation of child participation principles, exposure to these activities influences children's understanding and expectations of their participation rights. In Australia, children (unlike adults) defined obligation and responsibility to others and were challenging adult notions.

Differences within countries

Across the region, differences in children's participation that were related to culture, political regimes, socio-economic status, and history were easily identified. However, differences within countries were just as important and alerted us to tensions around children's participation that exist even within countries. These were generally associated with social positioning as it related to age, gender, income, rural and agrarian location, and caste, but were also the result of dynamic social relations and impacts of globalisation

In Sri Lanka, for example, adults in NGOs differed from other adults interviewed in considering that child participation had a role to play in creative problem solving. The Western ideologies underpinning the NGO structure included a perspective on the rights of children to participate that was not necessarily shared with those outside of the NGOs. The data from China indicated a generational conflict in which children were beginning to challenge traditional adult authority. It identified more areas in which they should have agency in decision making. In particular—in contrast to their parents—some children in China argued they should make their own decisions about peer relationships. The data from Australia also showed a generational conflict, with adults generally limiting children's participation to what could be labeled as 'youth issues', whilst young people saw they had a responsibility to contribute to a much broader range of issues.

Across the region it was generally the case that the older children were afforded greater and more diverse opportunities for participating. It was generally seen that children from agrarian communities were more likely to participate in authentic community activities than their urban counterparts and, in all environments, the more articulate children were afforded more opportunities to participate than the less articulate. It is clear that within countries the category of 'child' was not monolithic and children of different ages were differentially participating.

Importance of understanding power

This research has underscored the importance of an understanding of power in an exploration of participation as a right. The research in this region has shown how Western liberal assumptions about who has power—such as the expectations that adults will always have power over children—do not necessarily hold. In working with researchers from Eastern cultures and in the Asia-Pacific region we have been able to expose some of these assumptions and become aware of misunderstandings that flow from them. For example, when a country is racked by civil strife, torn apart by unrest and under threat, how does one understand power and who holds it? To discuss participation in such an environment in the same way as one would understand it in a stable political environment is inappropriate. Similarly, to talk about individual power in sites where collectivity is essential to survival has limited meaning and is, at best, simply misguided. Frameworks developed in stable Western democracies need to be treated with caution when applied to very different environments.

The acknowledging of difference

In conducting this research every effort was made by all country researchers to be open to the many ways in which children's participation was occurring in the participating countries. Through the practice of spending
time in each country and through constant reflexivity the team attempted
to be sensitive to its assumptions about what children's participation was
and to endeavour to be open to the participation that was occurring. Despite these efforts there is still a sense in which the project has been contex-
tualised within an overarching and dominant Western-liberal discourse of
child participation. The reality is that all discussions were held in English
and that the language of a dominant discourse constructs child participation in a particular way. The texts we used to explore the issue are all written in English and data presented for analysis was in English. It was expected that subtleties in meaning would be sacrificed but we were not prepared for the extent to which the use of English would obscure whole cultural frameworks. One example of a disjunction of meaning occurred when
the Thai researchers explained that a good and obedient child was seen as
participating in the life of the family. We cannot know the extent to which
equally sweeping understandings of participation remain hidden to us because of the differences between languages and cultures.

Where a principle has been recognised globally by all countries there
needs to be dialogue about how countries adopt this principle. In the spirit
of the UN convention, this dialogue needs to be inclusive of children. Each
of the five countries in the study was relating and responding to global
trends, pressures and opportunities, but they were not all responding in the
same way. Change is occurring in each of the cultures and countries studied
and each country is embracing change in its own way. The lesson to be
learnt from this study is that the success of UNCROC will not be meas-
ured by an outcome, but by the extent of each country's engagement with a
process. Before any real evaluation is made we need to more fully understand cultural interaction and the manner in which children are included.
It would seem that, to a large extent, the degree to which participation is
practised mirrors the relationship within that country between children
and adults.

In many ways the implementation of UNCROC amounts to a social
transformation. However, the imperialism or imposition implicit in the expectation that democracy is the shared and, indeed, only paradigm in
which this can be achieved must be questioned. The research reported here
has suggested that more needs to be understood about how countries engage with the UN convention, in ways that honour its intent but are culturally appropriate and country specific.